"May many become encouragers, thus opening up the potential for those encouraged to step forward with their God-given gifts instead of letting them lag or deteriorate. *The Barnabas Way* will help you fan into flame your God-given gifts."

—KENNETH N. TAYLOR, chairman of the board,
   Tyndale House Publishers

"For years I lamented my apparent inability to discover the big plan for my life. Only when I let go of the big and turned my attention to the small, seemingly insignificant events of life—the brief encounter here, the friendly conversation there, the unexpected relational connections scattered throughout my day—did I discover the blessed life I had longed for. *The Barnabas Way* is a profound reminder that at the heart of the Christian life is our call to be simple channels of God's love and encouragement to people in need. Thanks, John, for the reminder."

—LYNNE HYBELS, speaker, writer, and coauthor with
   Bill Hybels of *Fit to Be Tied*

"John Sloan has written a wonderfully inspiring and intensely practical book that reflects his own personal ministry of encouragement. John has played a pivotal role in my life, and his book will help you make a lasting impact on others."

—LEE STROBEL, author of *The Case for Christ* and
   *The Case for Faith*

# The
# Barnabas
AN UNEXPECTED PATH *to* GOD
# Way

## JOHN SLOAN

WATERBROOK
PRESS

THE BARNABAS WAY
PUBLISHED BY WATERBROOK PRESS
2375 Telstar Drive, Suite 160
Colorado Springs, Colorado 80920
*A division of Random House, Inc.*

Details in some anecdotes and stories have been changed to protect the identities of the persons involved.

ISBN 1-57856-575-8

Printed in the United States of America
2002—First Edition

10 9 8 7 6 5 4 3 2 1

*For those who showed me*
*the blessings of the Barnabas Way*

# CONTENTS

# INTRODUCTION

"You can experience a supernatural life with God." Plenty of seminars and books and conferences tie this promise to the blessings God gives. God's gifts signal his favor and love.

"Make God a daily part of your life—every day he'll bless you."

"You can know that God is active in your life; it will be evident by all that he gives you."

Does this who-wants-to-be-a-millionaire method of knowing God seem to be focused on the gift or on the giver? Does the challenge to believe God for bigger blessings shine the spotlight more on God or on what he does for us?

The view that rewards signify favor in a relationship lies at the heart of the 1975 movie *The Man Who Would Be King*. Based on a Rudyard Kipling story, the film follows Danny Dravot and Peachy Carnehan, two British soldiers of fortune who seek their destiny in the mythical land of Kafiristan. They find a civilization untouched by the outside world, a kingdom that's brimming with golden treasures. The native people immediately proclaim the Englishmen gods and crown Danny king, showering him with gift after gift and fulfilling his wishes and desires far beyond his dreams. Danny and Peachy would have liked things to stay that way, but ultimately the people of Kafiristan realize they've been deceived and take revenge.

We're a lot like the man who would be king in our approach to God. We want to live in a land where gifts and blessings are there for the asking. We see an abundance of blessings as a sign that we are still in the favor of God and men.

And yet the man-who-would-be-king approach to spirituality leaves some significant holes in the fabric of our faith. When we're out to seek our spiritual fortune, our concept of who God is changes. God is no longer the center. He's more like a force, an impersonal power that does things for us. But as C. S. Lewis notes: "God does not exist for the sake of man. Man does not exist for his own sake." When we believe God's whole mission is to serve us, we've put him in Aladdin's lamp and given him the name Genie.

God simply does not answer our prayers in the way we'd always like him to. And when we look at our side of the God-human equation and think about how we relate to him, not only does the search for blessings put a question about our motivation into the minds of our friends, neighbors, and those we work with, but what of those who ask for the tangible blessing of God…and never receive it? This latter group, those who are disappointed because the promised blessing never appeared, may end up feeling like Danny Dravot. Deserted. (In the movie, Danny is abandoned by every inhabitant of his one-time kingdom except for Peachy, who can only watch helplessly as Danny is forced out onto a footbridge spanning a chasm and then dropped into the abyss.)

Spiritual-life writer Gary Thomas says we've become a generation looking for ease and comfort and blessing. Is that what we're looking for? Is God present in our lives only when he does the spectacular or creates the big event? Or could he possibly work in paradoxically different ways, his interest fixed on all the little things and the average people, the insignificant and those who need another chance? Somehow, oddly, the latter is what Jesus seemed to prefer. And in the oddest of twists, this is the very way that Jesus pointed to as the road to blessing. This blessing, as we shall see, is better than anything we've been promised by those who say we can have it all immediately.

There's a major figure in the New Testament who loved God's blessings but who showed his gratitude for God's care by loving people, especially the overlooked and those down on their luck. His name was Barnabas. Who was he? His name is a hard one to keep straight for some of us. "Ah, Barnabas—yes, he was that rebel, that terrorist, whose life was exchanged for Jesus." No, that was Barabbas. "Wasn't Barnabas the Pharisee who came to Jesus at night and couldn't understand how to be born again?" Not exactly. That was Nicodemus. Barnabas was an apostle in the early church. And he is best remembered as an *encourager,* wanting people to remain true to the Lord with all their heart.

Barnabas's name actually meant "son of encouragement," and that's what he did, he encouraged. Nowhere is this life mission more stunningly played forward than when Barnabas stepped to the front of the New Testament stage to help two future spiritual greats— Paul and Mark—who came up against opposition or failure and needed to be encouraged to stand their ground. Barnabas stood with them.

What did Barnabas get for his encouragement role? In the Beatitudes, Jesus describes what will happen to a person like Barnabas, who was spoken of as "a good man, full of the Holy Spirit and faith." * Jesus made it clear that one who is pure in heart and one who is merciful will see and experience God—like Barnabas, who was singleminded about encouraging others and showed compassion to sufferers. This person is *blessed,* a person expressly favored by God. This is the one who sees God's blessings, the one who will find the riches of heaven.

Praying to be blessed? Or praying to be a blessing? Although it's easy to believe that the best way to get something is to ask for it, this book may be a surprise about how "receiving blessings" works with God. The best way to receive from God may just be to *give* to those who need help—as Barnabas did. An option that is open to any of us. Every day.

---

* References for all quoted Scripture are listed in the notes section.

## CHAPTER I

# THE BLESSING DILEMMA

⊠

Most of us have known people through the years who have looked for blessings, who have looked for gifts, who have looked for dramatic evidences that God was playing big in their lives. For many of those, the evidence hasn't shown up.

Who *doesn't* want to be on the winning side? And who *doesn't* want their leader to be the shining one, the exemplary one, the one with all the answers? That's the type of leader we often look for in God. As Philip Yancey concedes, "Sometimes…I wish that God used a heavier touch…. I want God to take a more active role in human affairs…. I want quick and spectacular answers to my prayers." When any one of us thinks about how we want God to treat us, the images are different, but they still describe God in terms of what he can provide or give. "We want, in fact, not so much a Father in Heaven as a grandfather in heaven…who… like[s] to see young people enjoying themselves."

We all want to experience the reality of God as our Father; no one disputes that. But when a person's view of God casts him in the role of always giving immediate answers and blessings, the lack of God's evident blessings leaves the disappointed with a couple of conclusions. Either they weren't praying right, or God had chosen to not bless them, in the face of his promises that he would. Many become disheartened and turn down the volume of their spiritual life. Some become angry and stifle bitterness in their hearts as they go on robotically attending church. Some become disillusioned and move away from their faith, looking back at God and his followers in the rearview mirror.

But it doesn't have to be this way. What if I could show that there is a secret of spiritual living that guarantees God's presence with us every day? And that God will bless us in ways that we could never imagine? And that it works every time? And that this secret can be ours whether we are young or old, rich or poor, the possessor of a high IQ or an average intellect, a person who likes to serve or one who's good at leading—this secret is for *all* of us.

These blessings are not reserved for those who think big, claiming descendents as numerous as the stars of the sky like Abraham. They're not waiting to be claimed by only those of bold faith, who walk like Joshua around the walls of what's to be conquered spiritually and blast them down. No, the blessings are much less in focus when we are first laying hold of this spiritual secret. But they are in abundance on the other side of belief and action. And God is near—very near—all the way through.

Let's turn things in reverse order, as they appear most often in today's search for blessing and health and a life of comfort. Blessings are first in view. God second.

## LIFE'S GOOD THINGS

Going back to my childhood, I can remember many more good things happening in my life than bad. But it's the bad things that I remember the most intensely, that touch me the most deeply. And it was at those awful times that God put some very special people into my life. Or to say it another way, at those times God came to me in one of his special people. And this person either planted a seed or watered a withering tree in my spiritual life.

Growing up in Los Angeles, I vaguely remember going with my dad to a Rams football game in the Romanesque L.A. Coliseum. It was impressive as a sports arena. I sort of remember trips to Disneyland when Walt Disney's amusement park in an orange grove was the only one of its kind anywhere in the world. This next memory is a bit hazy, but I remember going to Huntington Beach with my father and two brothers and making my way past the breakers by diving under the waves before they crashed. We swam fifty yards out from shore where the waves passed by in big swells instead of thundering down on us like avalanches.

I have these good memories. But my mind doesn't hold on to their details, and I don't think I was very much affected by them in the long run.

Yet I remember the day my father died like it was yesterday. I was eight years old. I felt the world slip out of its course. I thought there would never be another hour of happiness in my life. But at that moment a series of men began to appear, one after the other, who by simply being there for me kept putting the hope in my heart that God was still alive.

## THE SIGN OF GOD'S BLESSING

Blessings today are equated with happiness. Gifts from God are often seen as proof that God loves us. And there is great emphasis in certain circles on praying that God will bless us, increase our successes, add people to our churches, and demonstrate in fantastic ways that he is at work in our lives.

When pointed in this direction, our spiritual compass is not fixed on True N (True North) but on True B (True Blessing). And if the anticipated blessings don't appear, the unfortunate conclusion reached by some is that they just weren't praying enough. Or they weren't praying the right prayer. Or they simply haven't learned how to be spiritual. The daily orientation for this type of spirituality is the pursuing of and the claiming of "good" things, the "happy" things that we can attribute to God and celebrate with great joy. It's exciting for those who see the desired results, but too bad for those who don't see such blessing. Their lack of success threatens to invalidate the "ask big, he'll give big" thesis— their lives don't become illustrations in sermons.

I had a colleague in the business world whom I sat across the table from when it was time for our companies to negotiate. We were at opposite ends of the deal. If he represented his client well, my company would end up yielding contract points or money or both. If I were able to present the better argument, then he and his client would need to yield points in favor of my company. Good recipe for a fight and hard feelings, right? No. And this is why. We knew before the briefcases ever clicked open and the notes ever appeared that Christ, and our Christian faith, needed to supersede the deal. This businessman was exemplary in this regard. When the negotiations moved into areas of disagreement, he remained calm. When it was time to square shoulders and make a point, he was pleasant. He began friendly and stayed that way. He lived his faith in the world of business.

In the fall of 1999, he died in a tragic airplane crash, leaving behind a wife and four small children. In this nationally covered air tragedy, some celebrated sports figures who perished in the accident were mourned across the country. My friend's name was not that of a well-known athlete, but his family and all who knew him mourned his great loss, for they knew the type of man he was.

The "blessings theology" popular today says God rewards those who ask. But how does that explain a mother and four children who today have no husband or father? This couple had asked the blessing of God upon their family continually. God rewards all those who ask, so what went wrong?

## LOOKING FOR THE BROKEN HEARTS INSTEAD OF THE BLESSINGS

Think back to what has meant the most in your spiritual life— the nice things prayed for and received or the tougher things you have faced in your own life and in the lives of others. Choosing the first might mean avoiding my friend's widow and anyone else who has suffered loss, because their tragic experience doesn't square with a life filled only with blessings.

But pursuing the latter course—trying to help and encourage those facing the tougher times—means uncomfortable involvement with heartbreak and discomfort, and getting used to not having anything to say to the hurting, and having to trust that God remains a good God in spite of a world that festers with hurt and mistakes and brokenness. C. S. Lewis says the Christian view is that this is a good world that has gone wrong but still retains the memory of what it ought to have been.

My wife and I were barely acquainted with a family in our town who had a fifteen-year-old son and two younger daughters. In fact, we knew the boy better than we knew the parents. The boy wanted to be a writer, and since I work in the publishing business, he would bring his writing to me for my evaluation. I never knew he had a struggle with depression; he kept that secret from me. I found out later that his parents had been getting him medical treatment and counseling. But as is sometimes the case in these situations, on the last day of his life he projected a radiant optimism to his parents and to everyone in his school. He helped at his favorite charity that afternoon. And that night he took a gun and ended what had become for him an unbearable and seemingly unwinnable emotional struggle.

When we heard the news, my wife and I couldn't stop thinking about our young friend, and about his parents. So I went to them. I wanted to tell them I was sorry. I wanted to tell them that my father, too, had ended his life with a gun. And I wanted to just tell them we were around. I took them a pound of coffee. When I went the first time, the mother wasn't capable of coming to the door. Over the next few months my wife and I asked the couple a few times if there was anything we could do for them. We asked them to neighborhood gatherings; we asked them to go out to eat.

Initially they just weren't able to do anything. The hurt was too great. But eventually they asked us over for brief periods. We took some walks together. And I accepted their invitation to go with them to a support group for survivors of suicide. We really don't know what we did ultimately that was helpful, but months later at a conference we heard them tell a group of people that we had helped pull them out of the despair they had faced. And they'd felt God had brought us to them.

Looking back, I realize that they brought God to us. We were at a loss as to what to say because there are no words that can be said at such a time of painful loss. So we begged God for help. And he came to us. That was the biggest blessing. It was all because we wanted to encourage someone.

This experience begins to reveal the blessing that Barnabas enjoyed. In the context of Barnabas-like spirituality, two people can *both* be helped when one lends a hand to the other in the middle of a tough situation. This truth is mythically but realistically illustrated by the movie *Hoosiers*. Norman Dale, played by Gene Hackman, is a high-school coach seemingly without a past. He comes to the small Indiana town of Hickory to try to work the magic of making the school basketball team into a winner, maybe even a contender at the sectional playoffs. For Indiana, this is about as sacred a quest as Arthur searching for and finding the Holy Grail. Dale is opposed by parents of the players and other adults who think they know better what coaching a basketball team is all about. And winning over the players to Dale's way of playing is just about as hard a task.

Into Coach Dale's life drops Shooter, played by Dennis Hopper, a former Hickory Huskers basketball star who happens to be one of the players' fathers...and also the town drunk. In exchange for Shooter's vast knowledge of the players and teams and strategies they will face, Dale offers Shooter a job as assistant coach. With one caveat. Shooter's got to get and stay sober.

Dale forges an important bond with Shooter, who supplies the Huskers with good scouting and takes the first real, though not perfect, steps toward conquering his lifelong problem of alcoholism. But Dale also benefits from his relationship with Shooter in a way other than basketball statistics. Most of the town had seen the coach as a cold, unfeeling personality when he first arrived. But after his efforts with Shooter, people found out just how thoughtful a person Coach Norman Dale was. He finally received the support that he needed. That's the way it can be in real life, too. We reach out to those we think need help, and in the process of giving that mercy, we ourselves are helped. Which is the great paradox about the life of encouragement.

The most remarkable aspect of the Barnabas Way is this: It works whether or not a person knows the right spiritual technique or the right prayers or the right answers on the Bible quiz. Even for those in the worst of life's situations, who feel like what Philip Yancey calls "neglected saints, who learn to anticipate and enjoy God in spite of the difficulties of their lives on earth." These find true blessing because, "In their lives, the Beatitudes have become true."

This, then, is the experience we can share with Barnabas, the man who made his name in the life of the first-century church by believing in and encouraging a professed persecutor of Christians named Saul (later called Paul) when nobody else would. Barnabas, the person who slipped in alongside those who needed help and encouragement and those who had failed and became the blessing that so many were seeking. Barnabas, the one who ignored logic when choosing his candidates (John Mark) for "most likely to succeed" at getting back into the saddle again. Barnabas, the one who believed what his eyes told him he could not. He is the patron saint of those who give and of those who need encouragement.

## CHAPTER 2

# THINGS AREN'T WHAT
# THEY SEEM

※

Praying for power in our spiritual lives, praying that our ministry would grow, praying that our influence for God would be as great as that of a well-known international evangelist, even praying for broader resources for ourselves and the kingdom—isn't this what we should pray for and expect our lives to be like, if we only believe?

And yet success is not always measured in the spiritual realm as it is here on earth.

Praying and asking God to bring us someone who needs help, or praying for someone who represents another responsibility for us to find time for—this seems illogical.

But things aren't always what they seem to be.

One of the oddest things going in this life is God's chosen method for getting his message out to people: me and you. "Men are mirrors, or 'carriers' of Christ to other men." Either we reflect back to others what they truly are when they see Christ in us, or we infect them with the "disease" of Christianity. Now, knowing what

I do about myself, I see the human factor in the communication of God's truth as one of the weakest links in the system he designed. If we had the most important message for the world, we would take advantage of our best, most efficient, highest tech, and most foolproof form of communication to broadcast that message. We certainly wouldn't leave it up to imperfect creatures like us. And yet this is the method God has chosen. It's just not the way it should be; it is a paradox, something that contradicts our reasoning.

Different writers have defined paradox in different ways. In one essay, popular English writer and theologian-philosopher G. K. Chesterton referred to God turning his truth "altogether upside down." In another spot Chesterton spoke of God's delight in riddles that, by the way, "are more satisfying than the solutions of men." C. S. Lewis noted that it's a paradox in this life that what seems to be good to us may not be good in God's eyes, and what seems to be evil may not be evil; our black may be God's white and vice versa. More recently, author Robert Farrar Capon refers to God's paradoxical conclusions in the parables of Jesus and in the gospel itself as standing every one of the first-century followers' expectations and ideas about Jesus on its head. Using baseball terminology in another passage about paradox, Capon speaks of God's long, slow curve starting to curl in over the plate.

## THREE PARADOXICAL EXAMPLES

A number of paradoxes have appeared in my life in the past year. I grew up in California and Texas, two places as different as they can be. I spent most of my growing-up years in Texas, however, and made friendships there that will never end. One of the guys I became friends with about the time I turned ten was Ted. He and I would climb trees, ride bikes through the alleys, root around in other people's garbage cans for treasures, and build scouting posts in trees where trunks split and formed Vs, hammering two-by-fours between the tree forks as platforms to stand on.

As we grew older, our paths diverged like a forked limb in one of those trees, mine going toward sports and Ted's into other pursuits, each of us with our own crowd. But we stayed in touch, up through high school. When we last saw each other before we headed to college, we were still going in different directions. And we had a common attitude that though our paths were aimed toward different compass points, we were both *not* going toward that God-enterprise that had overcome a few of our classmates. We graduated in 1970, a time ripe for college unrest, antiwar demonstrations, and Jesus people. We figuratively waved good-bye and loped off as solitary riders, convinced our destinies were our own.

Many years went by before I heard from Ted again. During that time, I decided to investigate true Christianity. And I discovered it was true. I found out my destiny was not my own anymore, thank heavens—literally. Ultimately, after studying English and theology, I started work in religious publishing, which I've been a part of ever since. I've had the opportunity to work with many excellent Christian writers of our generation, people who can communicate God's truth in stories, images, and personal narratives. I don't see how I ever could have believed that Christianity isn't true.

Then recently I heard from Ted. But not directly. One of the authors I work with received a letter from Ted, in which Ted asked if the editor the author had mentioned in his most recent book's preface might be a fellow who grew up in northern Texas. The author sent me the letter, and I wrote to Ted. He's been down a rough road. He has an illness that very nearly has taken his life. He gets treated with different chemical potions that are supposed to keep the illness in check. He says the treatment works, but it does a lot of other things to him that he could live without. Same humor, same Ted. Except for one thing. Ted also has become convinced that Christianity is true. And the author he had written to, and whose work I edit, is Ted's favorite.

Now the paradox is this. If I had been scripting this story, Ted and I would have stayed together, or at least near each other. And after God had convinced one of us of the merits of Christianity, then God would have used him to persuade the other of the truth. Much more efficient. Much more straight-line. And my scenario doesn't have the obvious drawback that things can go awry when people who are influential with their friends are taken out of their friends' lives. Obviously I'm not looking at this the way God does, because he turns things upside down and arrives at truth. Ted and I have been separated by fifteen hundred miles most of the last thirty years, we both thought the other was still headed in the wrong direction, and God still communicated to both of us. It's a paradox the way he did it.

Paradox number two. I got to know a guy at a luncheon a couple of years ago. I should say, he got to know me. Mark saw me standing all alone at one of these affairs I really don't like to go to. It's the awkward event where you're invited to a lunch in order to meet folks from the business community. Somehow all the human chemistry supposedly ensures that you'll make the contacts you need and everyone will be happy.

Looking back on it, considering Mark's circumstances, I don't know why he was there. Mark has a neural disorder that is degenerative, and he has lost some ability to control his motor skills. At times he moves involuntarily and irregularly. At the luncheon he was not in a position to be shaking hands and impressing potential business partners. He would have done that better at the end of a telephone line.

But there I stood, hands in pockets, approached by no one (not even the man who invited me), receiving no greeting until… until Mark walked up and began a conversation with me.

I only met one other person that day. And that was Bill, whom Mark introduced me to. Bill wasn't as tall as Mark; in fact, he was stooped. Bill's head was a bit misshapen on one side too, and he talked in almost a whisper. Bill was recovering from the removal of some tumors in his brain. The neurosurgeons had needed to remove the back part of his jawbone and tamper with some of the nerves that affected his voice. That didn't stop him from extending me a warm greeting. But I'm sure the three of us weren't the business community's idea of the Welcome Wagon and its slickest crew. I could tell that by the way most people veered in a wide arc around us as we stood talking before lunch.

My view of making the very best impression is to use your

most impressive people. Mark and Bill didn't fall into that category. And yet no one could have made a better impression on me. It is a paradox. Once again I find out my black may be God's white, and vice versa. I never went back to another of the business luncheons, but I did become friends with Mark and Bill.

The third paradox is a hard one to describe. Sometimes I still can't bring myself to agree to its truth. I question why it had to happen the way it did. Wasn't there another way?

Over a period of ten years, a family my wife and I knew suffered three tragedies. In the first the husband and father died mysteriously, under conditions described as "suspicious," but the police were never able to uncover a motive for a crime, so the family learned the term "accidental death" and felt empty and ignored and angry.

A few years later the youngest son died of an illness that could have been diagnosed and treated if the illness had been detected. But it wasn't, and the family's bitterness grew. Finally at the end of this decade of pain, the oldest son disappeared in a boat off the Oregon coast. The boat drifted in to shore, but the boy's body never did. The last three family members, the mother and her two daughters, sealed themselves off from friends and other relatives, pushing away anyone who talked of optimism or faith or any kind of god.

Today that family sees things differently. Both daughters work in some form of ministry, one as a missionary and the other as a church's Christian education director. The mother travels between her daughters' ministries in the United States and Africa, helping her girls serve the people with whom they live. How did this happen? The answers of the three women differ only in their narratives. Each woman in some way says that the tragedies ultimately caused her to ask why of the only Answerer of those kinds of questions. And though what came back never really were answers, the time they spent with God led them into a relationship with him. And that, in turn, led them into the lives of others.

It seems to me that this can't be the only route to authentic belief. But then I'm not standing ideas on their head or throwing what appear to me to be long, slow curves. Things here on earth are not always what they seem to be. That's the paradox.

## A PICTURE OF PARADOX FROM PHYSICS

The best example of things not being what they seem to be comes in the world of physics. Everyone knows that Albert Einstein came up with his theory of relativity expressed by the equation $E=mc^2$, which led, among other things, to the making of the atomic bomb. Einstein did his work under the assumption that matter is made up of subatomic particles, held together in some jittery way in the quantum world. And Einstein believed, as did everyone else at the time, that there were three spatial dimensions—length, width, and height—plus the fourth dimension of time. That is what most of us learned in school.

But things are proving to be different. Instead of the smallest parts of the universe being tiny particles, it is now believed that the building blocks of the universe are strings, loops and loops of vibrating strings, which has given rise to a new name for this brand of theoretical physics: String Theory. And reality is proving to be even more unexpected than that. Instead of four dimensions, there are now believed to be eleven. And science doesn't quite know how to deal with all of them.

From particles to strings; from four dimensions to eleven. Things do not always stack up as logic tells us they do, as our minds want them to. As the years go by, we get more light, and sometimes more understanding, and we might begin to see that logic doesn't always serve us in comprehending the spiritual realm.

## BAD MATH

The Barnabas Way doesn't do well with numbers, another paradoxical problem for those wanting a quick return on their prayer investment. In fact, great addition and multiplication are never guaranteed and are seldom experienced—contrary to the expectations of blessings theology. Ministries aren't always expanded, followers multiplied, or horizons broadened.

No, the Barnabas Way generally puts a minus with another minus. In normal math, that produces a minus two. Here's where the paradox begins to turn, though. Take one person who isn't looking for his holdings to grow or his borders to expand, a person who might be below zero on the visionary scale, but who does have time for others, and add to him a person who is in some kind of need, who is also seen as a minus, and what do you get? With the Barnabas Way, you get plus two. I said it was bad math.

Put people together like the two I just described, and a magnetic attraction occurs. They walk together. Hurt together. Lose together. And ultimately win together. They are not big in numbers. It's a movement of two. It is an encounter not with impressive numbers but with significance.

Bob Buford, a retired cable television executive, has written about this type of encounter. He tells story after story of those who have made big money, counted big numbers, in the first half of their lives. And then they discover that they left out of their lives the one thing that is significant: people. Another person who has discovered the secret of helping just one kid at a time is Bob Muzikowski, an insurance executive living in Chicago. Muzikowski has started Little Leagues in inner-city Chicago and New York and has built the leagues focusing on one player or one adult coach at a time, letting players live in his home and getting them back into school and then into college when their youth baseball days end.

## THE BLESSINGS OF PARADOX

We live in a world where paradox is not seen as a valid explanation for solving problems. It is a curiosity among the choices we have for understanding any of life's unexplainable realities because it offers no empirical proof. And yet, with the contradictions, the bad math, and the descriptions of God's unpredictable ways of doing things, paradox prepares the way for a better understanding of Barnabas…and Jesus. They both worked at spreading the message of God in a less than straight-line, power-praying format, and more in ways that seemed odd and slow and…upside down, if a person is serious about getting the job done. That life, which is demonstrated in the Beatitudes—peaceful, pure, merciful, righteous, meek, mournful, poor in spirit—and lived by a Spirit-guided man like Barnabas, who reaches out to help others, may not be flashy, but paradoxically it is the way God works.

But here's where the paradox begins to bend back on itself. Even though personal benefits from the Barnabas Way seem so small compared to the gifts that some say can come from asking God for extravagant answers, a spiritual windfall does result. "The Beatitudes reveal that what succeeds in the kingdom of heaven also benefits us most in this life here and now."

The benefits of living like a follower of Jesus with a Barnabas mind-set—showing compassion, reaching out, encouraging—are constantly sought after through popular Christian seminars and books. Yet they exist for free in the spiritual life. Some of these unexpected gains are

- a new focus on people instead of things
- an opportunity to watch God bless, but not because we demand it
- emotional health
- the joy of seeing people get back on their feet
- a front-row view of the Cinderellas in life who get an opportunity to start over
- a chance to help people discover their own happiness

- an antidote for loneliness
- the secret to genuinely discovering our purpose

A few other benefits that focus more on our relationship to God include discovering that God is just and fair, experiencing God's unconditional love for ourselves and others, and preventing ourselves from getting disillusioned about God.

If you follow the Barnabas Way, I can't promise that your circumstances will immediately change so that you will have more money or a larger ministry or a better quality of life. I don't think anyone can guarantee that you'll receive those kinds of blessings just by praying certain prayers.

I can't promise less trouble. I don't think anyone can.

I can't promise things will all make sense. No one can.

I *can* promise that if you look each day for one who is hurting, one who has lost something, one who needs encouragement from God, or one who wants the support of a friend, you will never lack for a divine encounter. Someone will be there every day.

And you will be his blessing.

## CHAPTER 3

# THOSE WHO WILL HELP
# US FIND OUR BLESSINGS

⬚

Robert's marriage caved in about the same time he received a dishonorable discharge from the military. That kicked his drinking into high gear, and soon he was adding drugs to the mix. In the middle of one of his deepest troughs, he began calling me for help.

I had known Robert for almost five years. He'd helped us get settled after our last move. I'll never forget that. But I still couldn't see what good it could do to jump into the midst of his life. He had failed many times, and, selfishly, I didn't want to be dragged down with him.

Robert decided for me about whether to get involved. His telephone calls started coming regularly for about a year. In the morning, the afternoon, and the evening. I offered him as many encouraging thoughts as I could, always with the realization that I, too, had struggled with discouragement, depression, and lack of direction. Soon a radical change took place in our conversations. I began to hear and see Robert as a peer, as an equal, and not as a person with hopeless problems. I began to realize that his problems and my problems were the same. In fact, they were the same problems that confront all of us.

There were those around me who didn't look approvingly on our telephone exchanges. Some members of both of our families felt it was a waste of time. Some in Robert's family even thought I might have an ulterior motive. When he later came to spend some time with me and my family, a few registered renewed concerns. That's the way it is with believing in people who have failed, though: There will always be skeptics watching. We have a hard time believing spring will ever overtake winter again.

Today Robert is happily married. He has a loving family, he enjoys his career, and, best of all, he relies on God and not alcohol.

As I think back I also remember how I tried to slip away from renewing my relationship with a person who had chosen the bottle as the most important thing in life. Because of my memory of my own time on the losing end of life, and maybe because of my own guilt about how he'd helped me, I didn't pull away from Robert. I ended up helping him, in spite of myself. And, as we sat together with our families the other day, I thought about what a trophy for Barnabas our friendship is.

## THE BEST AND THE BRIGHTEST

As we think about spending time with people, just who do we expect that God will bring our way? What does that person look like and act like?

It's only natural for us to watch for the best, the brightest, the most impressive, the most charming people to pursue as our friends. We're drawn to the attractive people, the ones who seem to have never failed. The most faithfully watched TV magazine programs and the periodicals with the highest circulations cover almost exclusively the lives of the stars and their families. We want to know everything about them and feel close to them.

The same is true for celebrities in the political realm. David Halberstam, in his book *The Best and the Brightest*, outlines the errors we made in Vietnam policy by relying on human intellectual talent throughout more than one presidential administration. And yet a premise of the book is that John Kennedy's "Camelot" drew to itself the top thinkers, the best strategists, the most capable political decision makers, and the most attractive group that had ever governed our country. Today many look wistfully back to those days as evidenced by the popularity of a television series such as *The West Wing*. We yearn for another group of dashing young princes to lead us. They are the leaders we want above us and near us.

In our neighborhoods and friendship circles a similar magnetism is at work. I'm much more likely, when I'm out walking, to stop at the house of the man who has the boat—and the lake house to go along with it—and strike up a conversation with him as he washes his Lexus than I am to knock on the door of the man who prefers to stay inside with his psychologically troubled daughter whose cries are heard nightly. The woman who heads the parent organization at the middle school and organizes our block parties is popular. But few of us know the single mother who's never in the neighborhood after dinner because she works a catering job at the hotel an hour away. And that Bruce Willis double who chops Harleys as a hobby and tweaks his friends' car engines in the shade of his front-yard tree looks like a governor with a crowd of aides at the neighborhood parties. Meanwhile, a sullen-looking woman stands alone at the same gatherings. She is married to the T-shirted landscaper with the fiery temper who is suspected of causing those bruises that appear on his wife's arms, and sometimes on her face.

It's easy to want to overlook the people who don't hold out promise as potential friends. They retreat from our advances anyway, so what's the use? These folks repel rather than attract. Or at least their circumstances do. If we get too close to them, they might pull us down with them.

Yet the sandwich boards they wear ask for help. Troubled looks accompany a couple with the teenager who sat at the police station the night before until he could call and ask Mom and Dad for bail because of a drug offense. Worry is seen in another family's eyes as they go to the convalescent home to arrange for a higher level of care in an aging parent's assisted living arrangement. Frowns pull down the faces of still another family as they push the wheelchair carrying their oldest child to the car for one of the unending cancer treatments that must be endured. Anger lies at the edges of a young couple's clipped public conversations until it can spew forth inside their home and divide them, using money problems, broken promises, and trouble at work or in the schools.

These images are not very promising signs for successful friendships. And yet these people can lead us straight to God. It is their need that puts our hand in God's as we reach toward them with the other.

## FOUR PEOPLE WHO NEED HELP

If Barnabas and Jesus were right, then at least four types of people appear underneath a sandwich board that bears a plea for help. They show up anywhere, live on any block or across the street, are a part of any community, and are always ready to lead us by the hand to the Father because of the struggles they face. These are people who have failed, people who have lost (dubbed "the losers"), people who have suffered tragedy, and people who just need a helping hand.

Doesn't sound like the best class of recruits, does it? These people will never be able to go out and pyramid-sell your franchise and push you upward, increase your following, or line up in columns of ten-deep soldiers who can make a mark on the world. Yet the New Testament narrative makes it clear that these are the people Jesus chooses. Rather than attracting to his movement the nice and the capable and the powerful, Jesus seemed to attract "such awful people."

Now here's a simple truth, but all of us may not buy it: We're all ogres. And it's our refusal to admit this that keeps us away from others, from truth, and from God.

In 1995, movie creator Steven Spielberg, former Disney

executive Jeffrey Katzenberg, and music producer David Geffen brought their talents together under one roof to form a massive entertainment conglomerate. In its first five years DreamWorks SKG made three animated features for the screen, one about talking ants, another about Moses, and the final one about the road to ancient gold, which was very similar to the Kipling tale about the two soldiers of fortune mentioned in the introduction. Then the company rested its animation image for a year, until 2001 when it released *Shrek*.

If you're wondering where I'm headed with this, Shrek, the film's lead character is—an ogre. He lives in a marsh, scaring townspeople, eating ghoulish meals, and minding his own ogre-like business. Until one day he hires out to the evil Lord Farquaad to slay the dragon that has taken captive Princess Fiona, a beautiful and unattached maiden whom Farquaad has selected to become his queen. Shrek's pay for rescuing the princess is Farquaad's promise to rid Shrek's swamp of unwanted company. That is all the ogre wants back—his simple, lonely, miserable existence. And yet before his adventure is through, Shrek will have fallen in love with Fiona, and all that stands between them is, well, his ogre-ness.

Without giving away too much of the plot, let me just say that Princess Fiona finds out that she is not really that much different from Shrek. So instead of saying we're all ogres, let me say it this way: We're all Shrek. We've all got shortcomings, we all have problems, we all sin, we're all troubled, we've all failed, we all need help—we're all Shrek.

In *Brother to a Dragonfly*, a disturbing memoir about efforts by whites to work with blacks for integration in the American South, Will Campbell tells the story about the death of one young white friend who, like Campbell, was following Martin Luther King's pacifist call for change. After an emotionally charged protest, a deputy sheriff had come up to Campbell's friend and fired a lethal shotgun blast into him. Though wracked by grief, Campbell was pursued by a man who, for Campbell's own good, continued to ask the hard questions. Were both of the men sinners? To this Campbell had to answer yes. Then which of the two men did God love more? Campbell's definition of God's love, and of the meaning of Christ's death, gave him only one answer. God loved both.

We're all Shrek, but God loves us anyway. All of us. The sooner we see this, the sooner we'll move closer to people, and people will move closer to us. All kinds of people, but especially the people who need us most. The people, paradoxically, whom *we* need most.

## WHAT HOLDS US BACK

In one of my first jobs I supervised the work that was sent outside the company to a group of freelance proofreaders. I was not that great at outside supervision, but the work load grew to the point where a staff for my department was needed. And I knew just who I was going to pick as my first staff member. If he would take the job.

Martin was a carpenter. He'd worked on the remodeling of

the small office complex our company had purchased about a year after I was hired. Martin could knock the heads on nails flush to the wood with two hammer blows. Without measuring tools he could site-in the horizontal placement of shelves and mount them so the leveler bubble floated in the middle. He could shingle in his sleep. He had traveled to other countries to use his carpentry skills in missionary work, and he was sojourning on the remodeling job until he determined what his next stop would be.

Martin always had a book in his hand during his off-minutes. He generally spent that time alone. Not known for his smooth social skills or classy appearance, he had the reputation of being a loner. When asked a question or drawn into a discussion, though, his comments were wise and deep. I sensed Martin sat on great reserves of knowledge that were waiting to be tapped. I had spent time with him, and I knew Martin had the kind of critical, evaluative talents that were needed in my department.

My supervisor greeted my choice positively, as Martin was well liked and the type of person our company wanted to help grow into another career. It looked like everything was set. Until I talked to Martin.

Martin looked down at his hands, folded in his lap, and shifted his position. He didn't look up at me. But slowly he said that he did not think he was the person for the job I was offering. In fact, he was convinced he was not the one I was looking for. I didn't debate him on his statements. But I did meet with him a few more times and finally portrayed the job in such a light that he said he'd give it a try.

Within three months Martin had my department organized, the work schedule evenly distributed, and the evaluation forms flowing like they'd never flowed before. Oh there were little details he needed my help with, such as handling certain personalities on the phone or learning to let the head supervisor's comments roll off his back. But he was so efficient and so skilled in his evaluations that, when I needed some time off a year later, I didn't even think about work with Martin at the controls.

Sometimes what prevents us from succeeding in the Barnabas role are the people we reach out to. Some people don't believe in themselves unless we're able to give them a little jump-start. But more often than not, "the fault is in ourselves," as Shakespeare wrote.

Many of us miss the Barnabas role because we're not consciously aware that such an opportunity exists. We've not been looking for it. We've been alerted to Paul, Timothy, Jesus, and Moses. But where does Barnabas fit in? Where do we find his contribution discussed in places where the Bible is taught and respected?

Another reason why Barnabas slips beneath the radar is that his role is a quiet one, taking place behind the scenes. It is not one of the headliner acts or outreaches that gets front-page attention. But make no mistake about it. There are plenty of speakers and teachers and administrators who quietly act the Barnabas part.

I knew of one senior minister who communicated the teachings of Jesus from the pulpit as well as any in his denomination. But out of the spotlight we'd often find him devoting his attention and time to the older members of the congregation. These elderly folks had nothing to do with that minister's standing in the congregation. They rarely got out of their senior care centers, even on Sunday, and never exercised the power of voting in a church meeting. But he'd visit them anyway. (We always could tell he was at a particular senior facility by his trademark parking position. He'd drive by the many vacant spaces near the front door, thinking someone who would really need a closer space might happen by, and then he'd park in the far end of the lot, where no cars were.)

Some of us may not have developed the Barnabas gift because we haven't been convinced of its importance or need. Or if we have been convinced of its importance, the fact that no one has developed seminars to teach it has not caused us to sit around and lament the lack of an organized movement. There's too much to do based on this belief of serving others to worry about presentations and speeches and tickets.

## THE BARNABAS IMAGE

Allusions have been made about the cost in personal prestige that might come from imitating Barnabas. Some of those who are seen as being on the losing end of life are somewhat of an embarrassment to us and may cost us image points. *All* of us feel that hesitation. But perspective comes when we spend some time on the Barnabas Way.

A friend of mine I'll call Lou had a writing project that required him to spend a lot of time working closely with a woman named Marsha. This could have been an ordeal for my friend because Marsha had cerebral palsy, a disease that kept her very sharp mind locked inside a body that was out of control. Her words were slurred, many times beyond recognition. She tried in vain to keep her limbs from flailing about, and her efforts to walk in a straight line were usually rewarded by a drunken sailor's swaggering gait. Yet Marsha had brilliance of thought few knew about. She graduated from high school and college and pursued a lifelong dream in writing.

One evening Lou was with Marsha at an ice-cream shop. He wanted to reward the day's efforts with some strawberry or Rocky Road cones. He purchased the ice cream and handed Marsha her cone, and that's when things broke loose. Marsha began to get excited about the day's work, and the more excited she got, the more she began to sway and swing the upper part of her body. It was like she'd forgotten the ice cream was in her hand. Several other people were in the shop, some near the counters and some standing farther back considering the choice of flavors. In an instant every one of them began ducking for cover, not wanting to catch a ball of strawberry in the forehead.

Lou ultimately got Marsha's attention, and she calmed herself down, bringing the cone's movement into only a slight swaying motion. She looked around at the people and announced that her amusement-park body was meant for entertainment, not for war. Everyone laughed.

I saw Lou recently. He's worked with some of the highest profile people in the Christian community. But he often talks about Marsha. He sees his time with her not as an embarrassment or a shame to him but as time spent with one of the finest human beings he's ever had the chance to meet.

Someone asked me how to find the people who need a Barnabas. (And I would add, the people whom a Barnabas needs to be with.) He asked me if we were supposed to go looking for people in trouble.

We don't have to go looking for them. They're right in front of us. We just need to open our eyes.

## CHAPTER 4

# BARNABAS, THE SON OF ENCOURAGEMENT

※

Who is this man named Barnabas? According to Acts 4.36, he was also called Joseph, he was a Levite, and he was from Cyprus, the big island in the northeastern part of the Mediterranean, off the shores of Cilicia and Syria or present-day Turkey and Syria. I wish Barnabas would have stuck with the name Joe, since he's such a great guy, and Joe seems to fit a person who's always encouraging others. But the apostles called him Barnabas, the name that means "son of encouragement." Some translate the name to mean "son of comfort," which is also a good handle for Joe. I mean Barnabas.

Later the church named Barnabas a prophet, a teacher, and an apostle. Such a collection of gifts singled him out as a maturing believer, and one who as an apostle had been in the very presence of the Lord. As we seek to understand this man, there are four major landscapes in his life that reveal his character and his mission.

## LANDSCAPE ONE: THE COMFORT OF GIVING

In the first landscape we see Barnabas as one who gives. "[He] sold a field he owned and brought the money and put it at the apostles' feet."

Since Barnabas's home was Cyprus, the parcel of land could have been island real estate. And the land may have been inherited property. But Barnabas's gift was a demonstration of what had been said a few verses before, that all the believers in Jerusalem were of like heart and mind, they shared all their possessions, and they continued to tell about the resurrection with the great power of the Holy Spirit.

As a landholder Barnabas had some standing within the community, whether in his home city or in the group of worshipers in Jerusalem where he made his gift. And his first recorded act was to put his money where his mouth was, not just selling the land and donating part of the proceeds but delivering the full amount recorded on the title papers. Barnabas demonstrated that if we can give things away easily, then they don't own us. And we have our hands free to receive what is more important than money.

I knew a businessman whose story was the opposite of what we find with Barnabas. This man truly wanted to help people as he began his career in financial planning. He wanted to serve his few clients well and see if, by the miracle of God's Spirit in his life, they would see that something was different in him and would want the truths of Christianity he could offer them. As time went on, the businessman felt that if he could grow more successful he could attract more clients and give God's message to a greater number of people.

As the years went by, the businessman became very successful, had an extraordinary number of clients, and rubbed shoulders with the powerful and the famous. At last report his business is booming. He is getting into professional sports management. Hollywood is a regular stop on his West Coast itinerary. But his message has changed from one of faith to one of success. His words about Christianity aren't expressed anymore. His hands are filled with lots of prosperity, but they no longer reach out to people in compassion and with God's comfort.

Contrast this man's experience with that of Barnabas. He sold some land and gave the money to the church in Jerusalem. It was a simple act. Barnabas was not forced. But it signaled a lifestyle that majored in making room in his life for people.

## LANDSCAPE TWO: LIVING WITH THE ENEMY

Life in the Jerusalem church begins with Barnabas doing something totally within his character. He stood up and vouched for a new believer who was in trouble. This believer had been a known persecutor of the church, one high up in the Jewish religious hierarchy. He had been counted among the Pharisees. He was part of the mob that stoned Stephen. Barnabas defended this man, Paul (Saul), and affirmed the authenticity of his conversion.

But the church's acceptance of Saul didn't just happen like the flipping on of a light switch. His background made him the first-century equivalent of a Third World terrorist, hated and feared by Christians who dreaded his next act of barbarism. After the stoning of Stephen, Saul had gone to the high priest in Jerusalem to obtain letters of indictment of Jews in the synagogues of Damascus who had become believers. The letters would have enabled Saul to arrest and extradite to Jerusalem for trial any Jews who had become Christians. Of course we all know that Saul had a bit of an unexpected meeting on the way north to Syria. It was a meeting that changed his life forever.

The folks back in Jerusalem didn't know that. All they knew was that Saul was trying to jump into their Bible studies. The same guy who'd been muttering death threats not too long before now wanted to lead discipleship courses. The psychological profile didn't fit. So it fell to Barnabas to stand in the gap. (Barnabas actually stood up for Paul twice, once in Jerusalem, and then again up north in Antioch, the capital of Syria. It was in Antioch that the first Gentile church, and the source of all others, took hold and became the place Paul embarked from on all three of his missionary journeys. But first the Antioch church needed an introduction to a stranger from Tarsus. Barnabas again came forward.)

What Barnabas did was not easy. Imagine this assignment. It's 1960 in the American South. A man who waged a homicidal drive to inflict pain upon you and your friends because of your commitment to racial equality has just dropped by your house to tell you he's had a change of heart. Not knowing whether to answer the door with a weapon in your hand—since his hobbies have included cross burnings and late-night beatings—you crack the door just enough to see that he is unarmed. He says he really does want to make it right with you and those who have suffered because of his hatred. But he needs your help. You have heard that his violent crusade of hate has lost momentum and that his racist organization has fallen apart. You and your friends have thought that maybe he had a mental collapse. He had been a hatemonger. Now he is just a loser. And since the tide of public sentiment is finally turning in favor of civil rights, you can just turn the other direction and pretend the guy doesn't exist. But he has become a Christian, he says.

What will it mean if you accept this man's story? It will involve going to meetings with him where you will encounter fathers who have lost sons to his persecutions, mothers whose daughters have been abused because of his hate, humble people who just wanted to live like everyone else who walks upon the earth but were denied that right because of the prejudice of people like this man. You will have to face groups who adamantly believe the guy is not worth saving. "My daughter never got a second chance," one woman in your group will say. "This man caused so much heartache that we'll never be able to forgive him," another will shout. And in many ways you'll hear yourself agreeing with them. He doesn't deserve a second chance.

Would you stand up for this guy? Barnabas wouldn't hesitate.

All of the apostles were afraid of Saul, save one. Barnabas had heard Saul's story, and on the strength of Saul's words of repentance, Barnabas took him by the hand straight to the leadership corps, Peter and James. Barnabas told these Jerusalem apostles about Saul's experience on the Damascus road, Jesus' appearance to Saul, and how Saul had been preaching with great power in Damascus ever since. "He's changed," Barnabas said. "Give him another chance. I know he's been going from house to house in different cities and threatening every one of us who has become a Christian and dragging some out and ordering torture and death. But he is different. I swear it. And I stand here guaranteeing that change with my life."

We may say that it was obvious by Paul's change of life that he had become a new person, worthy of forgiveness. Why, if we'd been there, we would have defended Paul too. But we don't often face these kinds of situations, with the need to completely forgive and argue for those who need a second chance. This happened in the South in the sixties, and in Kosovo in the nineties, and in Palestine and Israel and Afghanistan and our own country today.

And yet what about the divorced person who remains isolated in the aftermath of a breakup and feels he has no place in his Sunday-school class anymore? Or what about the person who has been in therapy for months following several attacks of anxiety and now wants to come to the Bible study again but knows there have been whispers and questions about her mental stability? What about a guy who had been going to AA and working his program in the face of his twenty years of drinking but had dropped out of sight for several months? He called only last week, saying he was really going to make things work this time because he'd gotten back with the Lord. Then there's the friend who up until ten years ago had taught Sunday school and worked with the church youth group, but who started questioning his faith and had left his family and taken up with the wrong kind of people. Now he has come back to the community, and his ex-wife has been asking others to have breakfast with him.

The examples don't have to be as dramatic as these. Forgiving someone and taking his case to others for a second chance can be as everyday an occurrence as when a person makes a bad choice of words and needs someone to lead him back into the graces of the offended parties, or when one relative goes off on a family member at a holiday meal and needs a pathway back past the stern, stiff faces to the table, or when one child has broken ties with the rest of the neighborhood and can't figure out how to become part of the group again.

Giving someone a second chance is a dramatic picture from the life of Barnabas that Paul maybe forgot, as we'll see later.

## LANDSCAPE THREE: THE MISSIONS THAT BECAME POSSIBLE

The third and largest section of Barnabas's life circles around his missionary work.

Together in Jerusalem Barnabas and Paul received their commission to go to the Gentiles on what has become known as Paul's—not Barnabas's—first missionary journey.

Back in Antioch Paul and Barnabas put their gear together, exited Syria through the Roman naval base Seleucia, and sailed to the island of Cyprus, Barnabas's home. There they saw the conversion of a proconsul and the befuddling of a sorcerer. Moving on across a short stretch of the Mediterranean, they made their way into Asia Minor by landing at Perga, where one member of their party, John Mark, left them and went back to Jerusalem. Did he leave because of fear, a difference of opinion, or sickness? No one knows. But his departure created a rift between the two leaders, which we see after this missionary journey ends.

The missionary duo went on with the journey, traveling northward to Pisidian Antioch, where the good news/bad news scenario was a hearty reception by the Gentiles but a definite thumbs-down from the Jews, who drove Paul and Barnabas out. Eastward they went to Iconium, where they got more mixed reviews, but the old heave-ho in the end. On they pressed to Lystra, where a healing brought them the acclaim of gods. But there a posse from Antioch and Iconium caught up to them. Paul was stoned. Miraculously he was able to go on to Derbe the next day, the westernmost point of their journey. Then Barnabas and Paul returned home by going back through the same cities, through those same persecution-happy regions, to check on the planting of Christianity: to Lystra, Iconium, Pisidian Antioch, and down to Perga, and then across the northwestern part of the Mediterranean back to Syria.

Barnabas and Paul were together one more time at Jerusalem after that journey for public discussions about whether Gentile converts needed to add more Jewish ritual and practice (circumcision, the Law of Moses) to give them full standing within the church. But at some point after the Jerusalem meetings Paul split from Barnabas. It seems that Barnabas wanted to keep John Mark as part of their team, but Paul, having seen John Mark leave them on the first journey, did not want him along for the second.

It was a landmark split as far as Christianity goes.

It doesn't really matter what these two great apostles differed on regarding John Mark, whether it was his behavior or character or philosophy. And both Paul and Barnabas remained leaders who became torchbearers running across the Mediterranean world to Syria and Judea and Asia Minor and Greece and southern Europe to light the fires of Christianity throughout the known world.

But it remains a fact that the two men parted company. One stepped into the footlights of history as the visionary responsible for the three greatest missionary journeys of all time and is also credited with authoring much of the New Testament collection of letters. The other receded to the background, his arm around a failure of some sort, both of whom we last see in Acts sailing toward Cyprus.

I like to think about what that conversation between Barnabas and John Mark was like. As the crew unfurled the sails of their boat to catch the westerly breezes blowing across the Mediterranean toward Cyprus, John Mark must have been deep in thought. Maybe he was sitting on the side of the boat, watching the wake build outward as the ship picked up speed. He couldn't have felt good about what he'd just seen happen in Jerusalem between Barnabas and Paul, two stalwarts of the faith, and fathers of the growing churches they'd visited. Even if John Mark could have convinced himself that his sickness had been real and couldn't have been ignored or that his philosophical decision had been right to part company with the group early, still he had to feel responsible for the quarreling between the two men.

As he looked at the foamy waves working their way out away from the boat, I can see a shadow from behind him appearing and engulfing him and some of the waves he was watching. Right behind him I can imagine Barnabas standing, waiting to speak until the young man gave the invitation. John Mark would admit being down and wish he had used better judgment, and would ask if Barnabas wouldn't rather just go back and join up with Paul in the next missionary journey, minus him.

Barnabas would have just looked at his cousin. Instead of trying to debate the points John Mark had brought up, Barnabas probably would have just sat beside him awhile and looked out to sea. Finally he would have spoken. And he would have talked about the next trip they were going on, the things to look for in people they took the gospel message to, and what their goals would be for certain cities and certain regions. Maybe Barnabas would have talked a bit about the weather they'd be facing and the kind of outer garments to take along. And then he would have given John Mark a hug and moved off to the other side of the ship, never having taken up the subject of his young colleague's failure. It was the way the Encourager worked, and had always worked, leaving the mistakes of the past in the past and starting over.

## LANDSCAPE FOUR: THE UNREPORTED
## LIFE OF BARNABAS

If there ever was a segment of Scripture narrative left out that I would like to see, it's the missing scrolls on Barnabas. By that I mean the accounts of the rest of the work he did with John Mark and others whom we only have faint glimpses of in the New Testament epistles: a commendation here, a historical allusion to his work with Paul there, or a reference included in a greeting.

What happened with him and John Mark on their journeys? Paul got as far as Sicily and Rome. Did Barnabas lead trips farther north into Asia Minor, pushing toward the Black Sea? How did Barnabas and John Mark use what they learned from the disagreement and the decision to go separate ways? Did John Mark become an advocate for those needing a second chance, as Barnabas was? And were they ever able to put things right with Paul?

We do know the answer to that last question. Somewhere on down the way, Paul and Barnabas figuratively shook hands and went on with the work. We know that from four allusions Paul made to Barnabas in later letters, comments about Barnabas and him being those who had worked for a living and statements about their work in Jerusalem together. It's as if Paul just went on casually mentioning Barnabas, his good friend and able worker. But we really know the hatchet was buried by Paul's later references to John Mark. In three separate places, Paul affectionately refers to him, saying he is helpful to him and calling him a fellow worker. Paul may have forgotten that he himself at one point looked like a religious turncoat, but as time went on he saw the usefulness of Barnabas and how he could take the secondhand throwaways and make a space where God could make them useful again.

In the case of John Mark, had it not been for Barnabas's rescue efforts, we wouldn't have our second gospel.

Where was Barnabas when the end came for him—how many more used-up, washed-up, dumped believers did he take off the hands of those who wouldn't believe in them a second time?

Barnabas was a pillar for the beginning of the church's expansion in the first century. But he was also a man who twice in succession put his trust in what God could do with guys who had lost a lot and were not well thought of. Instead of building his ministry and asking for it to be broadened, Barnabas held back those who doubted the sincerity of a former church persecutor, and ultimately Paul's name has been lifted up as the Missionary Statesman for the last twenty centuries. Instead of jumping in with Paul on the postmortem of a guy who failed, Barnabas helped John Mark pick up the pieces with the result that there were two missionary teams, Barnabas and John Mark along with Paul and Silas.

His name never went up in lights, but for his efforts, Barnabas was blessed.

## CHAPTER 5

# THE BARNABAS APPROACH

※

The executive's desk looked like a landing pad for folders and stacks of paper. She had piled the manila mountains around the perimeter of her desk pad, leaving barely enough room to write. The margins of her typed-up notes were now filled with scribbling from the numerous calls she had made about a young executive named Eric Connally. He simply couldn't be as good as his résumé indicated, but every reference checked out. Connally looked good as gold. Sharp, aggressive, friendly to others, but a company loyalist, a detail person who could keep the big picture in view, a real worker who never made a mistake with outside accounts—and if he did he could cover his tracks. None of his former managers had a criticism to offer.

Rarely had she seen such a perfect product as Connally. As a corporate headhunter, she received a healthy fee to find the perfect ones, the real diamonds. She knew Connally would impress the firm she'd been working for over the last six months. It would be a match made in heaven.

But what if this headhunter had been Barnabas? Would the match have been so celestial? It seems that Barnabas, and Jesus, used a different set of guidelines for matches made in heaven. They chose people who had failed and recommended them for big jobs. They selected those who by the world's standards weren't sharp, and they talked to candidates whose past records of wins and losses mattered not at all when compared to their enthusiasm for the present mission.

Most headhunters would run from a candidate who wavered, failed, flip-flopped, backed down, or in some way showed he wasn't made of the right stuff. Barnabas, on the other hand, ran *to* them.

## How Barnabas Saw People

Barnabas was different from most because he, like Jesus, saw people in a different light. He saw people as they could be, not as they were. But how did he manage to see people this way?

One of the best places to see how Jesus saw God and people is in his Sermon on the Mount. Barnabas, Jesus' disciple and apostle, learned these same truths about seeing other people through God's eyes. The sermon talks about perfectly living the Law without one misstep, never thinking ill of those who are out to get us, making peace with our enemies, never lusting for what is not ours, turning the other cheek, and praying for those who have harmed us. But that's not all. The sermon also paints a picture of giving to those who have need, worshiping purely and forgiving others freely, treasuring heaven above anything on earth, believing God cares infinitely for us, avoiding judgmental attitudes, bearing good fruit, and building wisely on the qualities that last.

Who has done all of these things perfectly? God. And his Son. There are no more candidates. The Sermon on the Mount is a picture of God seeing us as we could be, as he wants us to be, since he wants us to be like him. Like his Son. We are works in progress.

But given that we are works in progress, how does God want us to look at ourselves and at one another in the present?

The answer comes in the Beatitudes, which begin the Great Sermon. A reversal is at work. We tend to look at the wealthy, the powerful, and the influential as the blessed and the happy. In fact, it is the opposite. God looks at the humble, the tragic, the meek, the honest, the tender, and the pure as the ones who can be truly happy.

Not many with these character qualities make it onto the *Fortune 500* leader list. They don't have what it takes. But they will appear on another list. The list of Jesus and of Barnabas. This list is one on which appears: The poor in spirit—those humbled by circumstances or who have laid pride low in their approach to life. The mourners—those who have suffered loss and seen tragedy and are heartbroken. The meek—those who don't try to step on their rivals or their friends to get to the top. The people who hunger and thirst for righteousness—those whose greatest desire is to do what's right. The people of mercy, who look for those who have failed or need a second chance. The pure in heart, the peacemakers, and the persecuted—those who stand up for peace and are willing to be on the side that sometimes loses.

Jesus viewed people through the lens of the Beatitudes. And so did Barnabas. This "window" on people showed Barnabas that it wasn't the wealthy, the powerful, the high rollers, or the popular who God saw could truly be happy and could reach out to others for him. It would be the failures, the second chancers, the people who'd had the wind knocked out of them. These were the people, in their struggles, for whom the Beatitudes had become real. These were the people who would be blessed. These were the people who needed God and would take him on to others.

## THE WAY IT WORKS

We've seen that Barnabas saw life—and people—differently. And he tried to view people as he held a picture of God and God's perfect responses in his mind. He tried to look at people the way Jesus did, guided by the Beatitudes.

But how did these beliefs become practice?

There are four general principles for implementing the Barnabas Way. They are almost independent of one another. They don't line up in any order as steps to be followed, but taken together they make up the Barnabas Way.

## Taking a Risk

Every Barnabas is always ready to meet someone who's not on the top of everyone's "have to meet" list (like Saul before and after the Damascus road experience). Following this first Barnabas principle means seeking out those who stand in the lonely corners of life because they don't think they look or act good enough to belong, having failed in the past or falling short in the present. Barnabas calls you and me to befriend this person, stand up for him, and spend time with him. It may mean sticking our neck out for him as we mentor him. It may mean risking our reputation, putting other friendships in jeopardy, opening ourselves to suspicion, or having others think we're just a little bit crazy.

A classic example of this is the late Tom Landry, the legendary Dallas Cowboys football coach. In the spring of 1979 one of Landry's friends was at the Cowboys' practice field and noticed an older, white-haired gentleman standing off to the side, his hands stuffed into his pockets and his eyes staring at the ground. The older man's head would pop up every once in a while to watch the practice drills taking place. Landry's friend asked him if that gentleman wasn't Woody Hayes, the former coach of the Ohio State Buckeyes.

Hayes had racked up one of the top win-loss records in all of major college football during his twenty-eight-year tenure as head coach. But he was fired from his position following an outburst of anger when he ran onto the field at the end of the 1978 Gator Bowl and slugged a Clemson linebacker who had just sealed

Ohio State's defeat with an interception. Not only was this game on television, but as a college bowl game, it was on *national* television, and the whole nation was watching. And those in the coaching ranks, the administrators and members of the National Collegiate Athletic Association (NCAA), and college officials across the country quickly moved to condemn Hayes's reprehensible action. Within a couple of weeks he was dismissed from all responsibilities at the university. He had given in to uncontrolled anger rather than serving as a role model for those he coached. He was, in modern terminology, toast.

"Isn't that Woody Hayes?" asked Landry's friend incredulously.

Landry looked up from his clipboard and across the field at the white-haired man, whose gaze was momentarily fixed on some linemen doing a drill, but whose head quickly and dejectedly dropped back down.

"Yeah, that's Woody," replied Landry in his easy Texas accent. Landry looked back down at his clipboard, but the visitor pushed further.

"Why is *he* here?"

Landry got that faraway look in his eyes that many during his coaching career interpreted as detachment but which often signaled deep thought and concentration. His reply was slow and measured. It was meant to convey information, not to hurt his questioner's feelings.

"Yeah, he really blew it," said Landry. "But he needs to be here. Somebody needs to give him another chance."

As a football fan I had seen the Hayes debacle on television.

As part of the national audience, I was deeply troubled by what he had done and felt he deserved firing and exclusion from the sport.

But Coach Landry knew what Barnabas and Jesus knew. Landry believed Hayes needed a second chance, and he gave it to him by simply inviting him to watch practice. Even though it was an unpopular move. Even though a second chance was the last thing many of us had in mind!

## Accepting Second Place

Besides giving a person a second chance, the Barnabas Way depends on the ability to push others into first place, ahead of us. Give them the credit in front of others. Let them receive the recognition.

Barnabas actually began the first missionary journey in the more honored and trusted position in the eyes of the leaders of the Jerusalem church. And Barnabas and Paul served equally on the trip. But do we ever hear of Barnabas's missionary journey, or Paul's *two* missionary journeys? The decision to avoid taking the credit is not very much like the up-and-coming executive who wants to be noticed in his pressed suit making the right call in front of the office corps and saving the day. Willingly accepting second billing is not very much like what happens in our Christian groups and churches either, sad to say. And though Barnabas is portrayed as the hero in this book, making the decision to let someone else have first place probably wasn't easy for him either. But Barnabas knew the statement of John the Baptist: "He must become greater; I must become less." When Jesus increases in our lives, we want to become less in the eyes of ourselves and others because we know he wants us to value others more than ourselves. Why must we "give preference to one another in honor"? Why are we told to "honor one another above" ourselves? Why are these qualities necessary in order for the Barnabas Way to work?

Most of us who need a second chance in life already see ourselves as ranking below every person we meet. What we need, more than anything else, is others having confidence in our work, the kind of confidence that comes from being recognized in front of others. If Barnabas had forever taken front and center stage, those he brought along beside him would have continued to see themselves as second-rate tools in God's hands, rusty old blades instead of brand-new Stihl chainsaws. Barnabas convinced them they had what it takes to be in first place, even ahead of an apostle such as himself.

## Remembering Who We Really Are

Right beside this principle of pushing others up in front of us sits a similar truth. If others do honor us, we shouldn't believe the press releases about how great we are. Having been involved in journalism assignments at a regional and sometimes a national level, I should be able to remember this simple fact: Somebody other than the athlete or politician or business executive writes the glowing press release. Lots of unflattering details get left out. The same is true with the "releases" written about me, that is, what others say about me. Somebody else gives me the public pat on the back. And they don't know me like I do. They don't know how great I'm not.

Remember when Barnabas and Paul rolled into Lystra, that city in the southern part of present-day Turkey? And how they healed a man with crippled feet? Did the press reports ever start flowing then! The crowd started calling Barnabas *Zeus,* who was the ruler of all the Greek gods. Paul they called *Hermes,* the chief press secretary for Zeus and the other gods. Now that could have gone to their heads. But Barnabas and Paul fully understood who they were. The healing was from God, not them. Their reaction was to rip open the front of their garments, a sign they were very unhappy with the crowd's response. They didn't want the glory. This quality of humility is demonstrated again and again in Paul, and it's one major reason why he, as a young believer, was able to take such positions of authority so early in his Christian life.

Almost no mistake is made more often in public Christian service than believing what others say or write about us. Working in the field of Christian publishing and with those who are known in Christian broadcasting as well as in Christian entertainment and public speaking circles, I unfortunately see the clay feet of some well-known people. The acclaim they receive can cause some to start believing the reports from a distance—by way of letters, published opinions, and broadcast media—instead of the close-to-home reports from family, friends, and lifelong trusted sources. Warnings about dangerous relationships, miscalculations in ministry plans, or personal burnout go unheeded as the unbalanced minister hears "Zeus" and "Hermes" from the crowd, instead of hearing a more objective assessment from those closer to home. The belief in the press report has prepared the way for the fall.

### Repeating It All Again

A final principle of the Barnabas Way is really a reminder. We need to round the final turn and then cross the starting line once again. After we complete a journey along the Barnabas Way, we need to go back up to the first principle and begin again. When someone becomes a disciple of Christ and continues down the road, it's not time to go on a publicity tour with our account of the difference we made in someone's life.

There is always another person waiting who needs our help or a second chance. That's what Barnabas did. After he gained acceptance for Paul with the leaders of the Jerusalem church, the case of John Mark presented itself. Without hesitation Barnabas moved right in beside John Mark. Had the writer of Acts followed Barnabas in his ministries after Paul and Barnabas split up, I think it would be safe to say that once John Mark got up and on his spiritual feet, we would have seen yet another Christian who needed encouragement walking alongside Barnabas.

## A COROLLARY TO THE BARNABAS WAY

There is a corollary to the four principles that define the Barnabas Way. I can't imagine Barnabas not liking it, for we know he continually put himself in the second-place spot. He let Paul move in front of him as the more able missionary. Barnabas was a Levite; he knew the Law. But at the time of committing his life to the mission of Jesus Christ, he immediately placed his needs second to the church and gave his land up for everyone else's good. Barnabas would have done anything to advance the case for Christianity. Including share a weakness.

And that's the corollary: Those who have failed, those who need an opportunity to begin again, are helped in their journey when we share our weaknesses and the stories of our own stumblings. If those who need a comeback only see our strengths, they won't know and they can't see that God takes brokenness and mends it.

This corollary points out who God will use for these missions of mercy, these privately sponsored restorations of collaterally damaged human "art" to their original states. God generally uses those whose hearts have been broken. God "comforts us in all our troubles, so that we can comfort those in any trouble with the comfort we ourselves have received from God." The brokenhearted are useful in God's hands because their hearts fall into the same little pieces again when they see similar circumstances of hurt in the lives of others.

In his book *The Jesus I Never Knew,* Philip Yancey tells of LaSalle Street Church, a congregation in downtown Chicago whose members include everyone from homeless men to Ph.D.'s from Northwestern University. It is a church whose doors are open to addicts and other "outcasts" as well as to the socially respectable. The church did more than open its doors, though. One formerly drug-addicted member named Bob spoke gratefully about the Alcoholics Anonymous chapter that the church invited to meet in their basement on Tuesday nights, cigarette butts, coffee stains, and all. It was because of that AA meeting that Bob started attending services and became a Christian. The people of LaSalle Street Church are people who hurt with sinners. They've been there. They're the ones God recruits to offer others a second chance, a chance all of us need not only before our conversion but after.

A couple I met very briefly in a community meeting were in deep pain and shock over the death of their child from a congenital heart problem. They were having a hard time just getting by each day. The wife's extended family didn't help matters when they invalidated the couple's extended grief by telling them they should just "get over it." This caused more pain and a shuttering away of that family's religious suggestions.

After a few more meetings the couple gave me the chance to share about my experience, and how devastated I was over the death of my oldest brother from leukemia when I was ten. This shared knowledge opened the way to many more conversations and ultimately to the young couple's interest in my reaction to the tragedy and how someone could move toward God in spite of such loss. The couple never would have asked me about my faith, though, had I not shared the heartbreak of my brother's death and the difficulties I had with it for the next many years.

Everyone needs a second chance. And it helps to hear about the way through failure and pain from one who has walked that path.

A second chance for people who need it was always high on Jesus' list. Even when putting together the team that everything in the world literally rested on. And with them he changed the world.

## CHAPTER 6

# THE REWARDS OF THE BARNABAS WAY

⬥

The inspiring motion picture *Rudy* is based on the experiences of Rudy Ruettiger, who grew up in a working-class family in Joliet, Illinois, vowing that he would one day play football for the Fighting Irish of Notre Dame. It is a story for all of us who love the underdog. Ruettiger lacks the talent both on the field and in the classroom that he needs to be accepted into the legendary school. But all he wants is a chance to earn the right to suit up in a Notre Dame uniform, step onto the field in South Bend, Indiana, and play in one play. Nobody thinks he has a chance—not his father, or his brothers, or even his girlfriend.

But Ruettiger gives everything that's in him to the quest. He can't qualify academically to enter Notre Dame, so he enrolls at a smaller school nearby, Holy Cross, to pull up his grade point average. The semesters come and go, and his applications to transfer are denied. His odd jobs weigh him down. His debts pile up. And he shoulders his burdens alone because his family and friends have turned away from him and his silly pursuit. If you're human, your heart just breaks for this guy until he finally gets accepted into Notre Dame. But then he hasn't even really taken the first steps toward making the football team.

Rudy becomes a walk-on at Notre Dame's practice fields, a nonscholarship volunteer who pulls on a jersey and basically serves as a blocking dummy, a padded target, for the Irish linemen to block and batter between games. Suiting up for target practice gives hopefuls like Rudy a chance to show their skills, and possibly catch a coach's eye, or so they think. But the odds on qualifying for a spot on the roster are so long as to be impossible. The scholarships that bring recruited high-school stars to Notre Dame are rarely voided.

Still Rudy suits up excitedly for each practice, going from one year to the next, giving everything he has, but never making the game-day roster of ninety. Rudy's finances get so low that he is forced to take a landscaping job to keep the football field in shape for the games. He can't afford a place to live and ends up sleeping on a cot in the stadium groundskeeper's office. Grades are even more difficult at Notre Dame than they were at Holy Cross. His family has basically disowned him.

I can still remember what I felt as I sat in that movie theater when Rudy finally made the game-day roster, when he finally got to suit up in the Irish blue and gold and run out in front of a packed Notre Dame Stadium with the rest of his team, in front of his school friends and, yes, even his family—his father and mother, and his brothers, who now had become his greatest fans.

"That's my son out there," Ruettiger Sr. boasts as he thumps his chest.

It's almost anticlimactic that, after a groundswell chant from the crowd, the coach puts Rudy into the game. He even gets in on a tackle from his defensive line position. Rudy has come from behind; Rudy has overcome the odds; Rudy the underdog has won. And as the team lifts Rudy Ruettiger to its shoulders to carry him off the field as *the* winner, I remember passing tissues between us and our friends and exchanging gurgled half-laugh, half-cry expressions of happiness and satisfaction about the great story we'd just witnessed.

We love to see the underdog win. If we're not there to see our home team, we'll root for the team that has the farthest to go and the most to prove. Every year in March, basketball fans—and even those who are only casually interested in sports—turn their attention toward the NCAA Tournament that will determine which college team out of the top sixty-four will work its way through the draw and win the final championship game and earn the title Number One. Another story that's just as important parallels the road to number one, and that is how far the Cinderella teams—the underdogs—will go. Schools like Princeton and Gonzaga, which don't have the multimillion-dollar sports programs, are in the chase. We love cheering for them, and we feel chills up and down our spines when they win.

That great feeling is one benefit of watching people face the challenge of life, especially if the odds are against them. When no one gives them a chance or after they've failed. And the person with a Barnabas-like heart enjoys only one thing better than see-ing it happen…that's being the one shouting the encouragement that helps make it happen.

## What's in It for Me?

Helping the underdog wind up on top is great, but what's in the Barnabas Way for me? Besides the great feeling we get when we finally see Rudy get to put on that Notre Dame uniform and play, is there any tangible benefit for the Barnabas who's standing on the sidelines cheering?

When we examined Barnabas's life in chapter 4, we read how his mission to the second placers, the underdogs, and the failures brought him closer to God, as promised to all who live the Beati-tudes. The spiritual benefits of helping others the way Barnabas did are apparent. But the benefits are as significant here on earth as they are in the spiritual realm.

Those who study human behavior say that the most pro-found sources of motivation in life do not come from feeling con-fident in ourselves, as the late-night infomercials would have us believe. The experts also say that feeling loved and belonging to a group aren't the most effective motivators either, as important as those things are.

In a great simplification of what these behavior experts say, human beings are motivated by a number of needs in life that arrange themselves like the rungs on a ladder. The needs that are on the lowest rung need attention first before we can step up to the second rung. Then the needs on the second rung need attention before advancing to the third rung, and so on.

The most pressing needs have to do with the basic human desires of wanting to satisfy hunger and thirst, wanting to find a safe place away from physical danger, and wanting to calm feelings of fear or anxiety. Next come the desires or needs to feel loved and accepted by those around us, then to feel good about ourselves, to gain more understanding about the world around us, and finally to find fulfillment in ourselves and what we do. Researchers discovered this progression simply by watching what humans do, recording why they do it, and watching what makes people happiest.

But there is one more level that is the most transcendent, the most profound level of all. What makes us ultimately the happiest and the most fulfilled is helping others find their own happiness and become all they are meant to be. This finding is based on research of human behavior and motivation, but it sounds a lot like the Barnabas Way.

## Why Do We Do What We Do?

Can the Barnabas Way give us the fuel that stokes the fire in our hearts and supplies the energy for helping others? Are there benefits from the Barnabas Way for us as well as for others?

We have already examined several spiritual reasons to go into each day looking for someone to help. But there are two big rewards that we enjoy beyond the spiritual benefits as this attitude lifts us into the highest level of personal fulfillment in life. Many of the personal rewards match up to the hierarchy of our need fulfillment described in the previous section.

## A New View of Life

The Barnabas Way can radically alter the way we view life. There is a diagram used by a Christian organization that pictures a cross sitting on a chair to indicate that a person has God in the right place, on the throne of his life. Another diagram pictures the cross off the throne. Now the person has taken control of his own life. He views everything through his own desires, wants, and needs instead of through God's perspective. Many would admit that's how we often view life, with our own desire for success or want of money coloring everything we look at, dropping thoughts of God back to second or third place. With the Barnabas Way as a guiding principle, however, we are constantly on the lookout for that next person who needs help. Is she a family member or a total stranger? Thoughts of hunting for a new sports utility vehicle or upgrading my wardrobe or finding a better mortgage rate suddenly pale when I've identified a human being in need of help.

When I was finishing this book, I was trying to juggle my personal writing deadlines, my work schedule, and my family responsibilities. I'd reached the point where I thought I was finally seeing some daylight. Then my wife and I, independently of each other, started thinking about some friends who live in another part of the country. Their last two years had been disastrous for them businesswise and personally. My next business trip

would take me through their part of the United States. And my
wife had a frequent flyer coupon. When she and I finally compared notes, we realized it had been almost ten years since the
four of us had last been together. We knew that our friends could
really use the encouragement. It felt as if someone had taken a
straight pin and pushed it into the figurative weather balloon
above my head, sending all my plans and schedules and expectations spewing out all over the place.

All of a sudden it hit me. Some people were in need, and
those people happened to be our good friends. Barnabas looked
at life and saw people. He would make the changes and go without giving it a second thought. In fact, he probably would have
suggested the change in plans a long time back.

"Would two weekends from now fit your schedule?" I heard
myself say after we got our friends on the phone. The Barnabas
Way sure changes how you view life. (By the way, I was able to
keep my work and personal projects on track, and we kept our
family time intact. Somehow we ended up with enough hours.)

Mental and emotional health are high on the list of things we
say we desire in this country. Yet seventeen million adult Americans
suffer from depression during any one-year period. The emotional
chains that bind people who get depressed—such as low self-
esteem, a pessimistic view of life—are broken by the life orientation of one following the Barnabas Way, since this person is always
looking out for what can bring happiness or a second chance in the
lives of those around him. It is also interesting that a person who is
depressed often struggles with feelings of hopelessness, sadness,

and a loss of interest in personal endeavors as well as activities with others. And yet a few of the recommended suggestions for self-help for the depressed are to find people to share thoughts with, to work at being with others instead of being alone, and to participate in social activities. A natural pursuit of one following the Barnabas Way is being involved with people.

An individual in a convalescent home complained of the depression he struggled with. His regular routine was to hurriedly eat meals, get back to his room, and then sit alone in an armchair and wonder why he felt so sad. One day on the way back to his room he realized that his next-door neighbor had been taking all of her meals in her room. And he remembered a nurse saying the woman was having breathing problems. Knowing the woman was well thought of in the dining hall, he suddenly considered dropping in on her and telling her she was missed. After stopping for the first short visit, he continued to drop by until she got well enough to return to eating in the dining room. Not only did the woman return to her place in the dining hall, but orderlies began to see a gleam in the man's eyes that hadn't been there for some time.

That's what following Barnabas's pattern can do for us. We see the joy of people getting on their feet. Each day can become a new day, an extraordinary day as we watch people find their own happiness or see them get a chance to do again what they've been wishing they could do over. And watching others whom we've encouraged get back on their feet puts a gleam in our own eye.

Somewhere along the way we realize, deep down, that following Barnabas's way fulfills our own purpose in life. Because this is the same thing that God does for each of us, every day. And we see God differently. We see that he is just and fair, as we now have a way to help those for whom life has been unfair and unjust. We see that God blesses, not in response to our command, but using our arms and legs in ways that have been right here all along. We have the cure for our disillusionment with God because we know where he is in the hurts of life, right here, with us, for others. And we feel his unconditional love, first for us and then for others.

When the Barnabas Way becomes our way, we offer others a second chance or a new start. But at the same moment, God offers those fresh beginnings to us, each and every time we hold out our hand to someone, through a new view of life and a new way of living.

## Being with Real Cinderellas

One more windfall from the Barnabas Way is that we end up being with the people who really want to be with us.

I'm not grasping for one last benefit. But it will take an illustration to make this one clear. On a Sunday not too long ago I was standing outside our church auditorium. A person involved in the church leadership came walking briskly by, looked right at me with a blank expression, and kept on going out the back door of the church. Busy with the day's activities, I'm sure. The door to the auditorium opened again, and out walked a businessman I knew who looked over the top of my head. The look of recognition in his eyes told me he'd connected with someone behind me, and I didn't bother to pull my hand out of my pocket for a shake as he strode by mumbling "hi" and brushing against my shoulder.

I walked over to the donut table and started to get a cup of coffee when I ran into my friend Mark, whom I introduced in chapter 2. Mark has a disease that's slowly affecting his nervous system. Side effects include a lack of control of some of his motor skills, which means that he has a bit more motion in his limbs than you or I would have. It's hard for him to hold a coffee cup still, or pick it up or put it down with ease. But the minute Mark saw me he greeted me with enthusiasm and did everything he could to get that cup down onto the table so he could shake my hand. Mark isn't the guy everyone gathers around after the church service is over. He isn't an elder. He's not meshed into the thick of community activities that put a small bunch of people at his side during the breaks on a Sunday morning. But Mark wants to be with me. And I want to be with him.

I was reminded of the same thing one evening at a banquet given for the people my wife works with. It's a great group of people. They're teachers. One person in particular, however, has impressed me as we've gotten to know the faculty and each of the teachers individually. Sherry is a single woman who teaches second grade. She's always involved in the group camaraderie and fun, never off on her own, but generally one-on-one in meaningful conversation. Of all the people in the group, Sherry's the one who has made me feel most at home when I attend a function, talking about professional hockey or a number of other common interest areas. And personally, I think she's a pretty spectacular human being.

Sherry has more excuses to refrain from going out of her way for others than most. Reason? She was born with Larsen Syndrome, a genetic condition that causes a slower growth rate and results in short limbs and stature. She is proportioned correctly, just smaller, at exactly four feet in height. But any group she's in has fun. Like at my wife's last faculty function, a Christmas dinner and dance. Sherry and Laren did the polka, and you should have seen Sherry and me do the swing.

The Barnabas Way has several different twists, the least of which is the opportunity to be with Cinderellas. Real Cinderellas. People who are so interesting and beautiful that you wonder how other people are able to pass them by.

## CHAPTER 7

# THE BEST CRITICISM
# IN THE WORLD

⬚

Life is funny. Sometimes those who seem to be our enemies are really our friends.

Take the scorpion. The venom of the five-inch-long "death stalker" giant Israeli scorpion contains chlorotoxin, a substance that seeks out cancer-causing cells in the brain and keeps them from traveling anywhere else in the body. This magical transformation of a death poison into a life preservation substance could be the answer for 25,000 Americans suffering from glioma, at present an incurable and swiftly lethal form of brain cancer. Then there's the copperhead, a snake found in the eastern United States. A protein in its venom markedly slows down the growth and spread of tumors, and medical science sees the snake's poison as a new friend because of its prevention of breast and ovarian tumors in lab animals.

A substance distilled from the skin of the poison-dart frog of Ecuador is a potent painkiller, two hundred times stronger than morphine. And from vines growing in South America, a substance known as curare can be extracted to poison the tips of arrows but also to make a muscle relaxant. Venom from the saw-scaled viper is used to make an anticoagulant, and various pit-viper venoms have molecular compounds that act amazingly like substances in white blood cells and fend off bacterial infections. Researchers are preparing to test them in the fight against everything from cholera to staph to strep to salmonella.

## ENEMIES TURNED REMEDIES

Medical science demonstrates that what in its original form can be deadly can also be turned back on itself to become a remedy, a healer, a friend.

The same is true for criticism from those who advocate a bigger-is-better approach to the Christian life. Some will say that following the Barnabas approach limits our trust in God and prevents us from seeking his biggest miracles. This view is especially prevalent in a day of widespread belief that we can have blessings for the asking. How can the Barnabas Way motivate us to dream a big dream and believe God for big results, since it's only concerned with one case here and there? Instead of praying a little prayer with a giant impact, the Barnabas Way leads its followers into the dead ends and quiet alleys of life and away from the great miracles God can do. This limits the gospel; it gets in the way of God's exciting plans for every Christian.

Such criticism could poison. Or, with God's fondness for turning things around and sending them in the opposite direction, words of criticism can produce the opposite effect and strengthen the people they were meant to hurt.

Appropriate and truthful criticism can point out error in any philosophy. If following the Barnabas Way would cause us to limit the gospel or hold back the believer from an exciting, wonderful, fruitful life, filled with miraculous answers to miraculous prayers, if it were a denial of the abundant life in Christ, then its application would be spiritually suicidal and its recommendation would be heretical.

The Barnabas Way doesn't mean that a believer settles for praying small prayers and believing God for little or nothing. We need to remember the name of the man who was 50 percent of Paul's first missionary journey. Paul's partner was Barnabas, the Son of Encouragement. And working together on that first mission trip, they set the course for the worldwide spread of the message of Jesus Christ. True and undeniable miracles of a first-class nature occurred on this journey. Barnabas believed God for the biggest miracle most of his peers could think of: He took a chance on a partner who had been a bounty hunter looking to turn Christians over to the Roman Empire. The miracles and global mission qualify this trip as having "big dream" character, big or bigger than any movement under way today. Barnabas was never lacking in faith or boldness or the belief that God works miracles in the lives of others.

In a positive way, when focused on numbers or bigness alone as the measurement of the success of Christianity, this criticism about limitation shines up the central truth of the Barnabas Way. And that truth is Jesus' emphasis on the individual, the lonely, the marginalized, and the hurting from whose ranks have come some of the most important leaders in church history, all because of the Barnabases who took a chance on them.

Criticism can point out loopholes in a philosophy. "The Barnabas Way doesn't work every time." That's true. That loophole has been with us since Jesus came to earth. And it will be with us until he comes again. Remember, one of the disciples who spent three years at Jesus' side ended up falling away. The diligent investment in the life of another doesn't guarantee success. At last count the only approaches to Christian living and discipleship that can claim 100 percent success from start to finish, in every follower's life, are nil.

But the most interesting effect of all criticism is that criticism only makes the headline type bolder when the critic is proved wrong. Numerous are the stories of Abraham Lincoln's slowness, insufficient mental prowess for his high office, deficiencies in formal education, and reliance on the low and vulgar manners of his upbringing. Yet historians universally recognize him as our greatest president, and this underscores his accomplishments all the more. The same is true for the two main examples in this book, a persecutor of Christians later entrusted to be the emissary and keeper of the faith and a failed Christian spokesman who got to try again and later penned the gospel of Mark.

## WHY IS THERE CRITICISM?

We create as many views of the Christian life as we do of Jesus himself. In academic books modern authors portray Jesus as a political revolutionary, a magician who married Mary Magdalene, a Galilean charismatic, a rabbi, a peasant Jewish cynic, a Pharisee, an anti-Pharisee Essene, an eschatological prophet, a hippie, a hallucinogenic leader of a mushroom cult. Some professional athletes see Jesus as a big defensive tackle, and a baseball player who breaks up double plays by sliding hard into the second baseman so he can't make the throw to first. We create our own images of Jesus, and we create him as we would like him to be. All of us would like to serve a Savior who insulates us against suffering and who sees to it that all our desires are fulfilled. No one likes to endure pain or poverty.

In March of 2001 the Discovery Channel carried an archaeological special that promised an accurate forensic reconstruction of what Jesus looked like, based on the latest discovery of male human skeletons from that time period. Their finding? The model of the human head looked more Neanderthal (low, flat forehead, wide-set eyes) than like a modern Caucasian, but our pictures of Jesus are most often modeled after a European or American white male. The model offered by the Discovery people was more like the skull structure of those in our present society with Down syndrome. In the physical appearance of Jesus as well as in the way we think he must have acted, we make our conclusions about Jesus with an eye toward what we'd like to believe.

The Barnabas Way can be even more interesting when it exposes the weaknesses of our assumptions about whom God uses (the gifted, the achievers, the beautiful). Henri Nouwen, priest and author, mentor, and distinguished university professor, spent the last decade of his life at the L'Arche Community of Daybreak in Toronto. Rather than finding a setting attuned to academics, writing, and study, Nouwen found L'Arche Daybreak to be a community linked to others throughout the world who are inspired by the Beatitudes. The administrators pair people who have a developmental disability with able-bodied "assistants," volunteers who come to serve.

Nouwen was paired with Adam, a young man severely retarded from birth who had to have every function taken care of for him, from all his hygienic needs such as bathing to needs such as being fed. He could not speak an intelligible sentence. Nouwen agreed to be his caretaker. And Nouwen's testimony was that Adam led him into a deeper relationship with Jesus Christ than he'd ever known before.

Nouwen also talked of times he'd take a community member other than Adam on speaking engagements. Nouwen would speak for an hour to groups who showed fairly good interest in what he had to say. Then he'd introduce his traveling companion, an adult with Down syndrome perhaps, who would get up before the group, tell them in a simple sentence that God loved him and each one of them, and then indicate they should love one another. And in a single moment the audience was convicted to a depth Nouwen had only hoped for with his own lecture.

God uses many people, and they're not always the people we would consider the most qualified for the job. Some of the biggest influences in my own life were the most criticized—a minister who refused to sacrifice the individual for the sake of church growth, and a family who devoted themselves to helping people pick up the pieces but did not care about their own shortcomings showing, for which they were roundly criticized.

## WHO IS THIS BOOK FOR?

Any book on finding blessings can be read in isolation, protected by a vacuum surrounding the reader. And we can think it would be good for *others* to behave like this, with the excuse, "I already do." In this book I've tried to use the first person singular or plural (I, we) throughout and stay away from the second person (you) because this message is for all of us. I know of no one who has mastered its lessons. We all have great room for improvement.

Actually this book tells us how to hang in there and go on with Jesus. If you have listened to popular Christian music, you realize after a while that every song is driven by one of three themes: going away from God, moving back to God, or continuing with God. Hanging in there. (Is this really a surprise? All music about a person in a relationship with another person is about these same themes. It is no different when God is one of the persons.)

Being a Barnabas—helping, loving, encouraging others who need a chance or a friend or both—helps us hang in there with

God. And we often find that those we reach down to are actually pulling us up.

The value of one human being reaching out to another cannot be overestimated. It is the core of the Barnabas Way. And its effects get painted in bright hues in our minds as we watch people helping people instead of using them or ignoring them.

African American journalist, poet, and teacher Patricia Raybon wrote a book called *My First White Friend*. In it she includes the text of a letter she wrote to a white girl, Kerry Monroe, who reached out to her when they both were fourteen years old and were students at Northglenn Junior High School in Northglenn, Colorado. It was Patricia's first year at the school where Kerry had previously been a student. The effect of Kerry's kindness was large in Patricia's life—and beautiful.

> Many wouldn't sit next to me. Or talk to me. Or look at me, except to point and whisper and giggle....
>
> So that first week at the Northglenn school lasted a year in my soul....
>
> When those four white boys in the lunchroom threw their sliced peaches onto the back of my head, and the sticky juice and the peach flesh clung to the curls that the beauty shop in Denver had so carefully pressed—and when the teacher on duty in the lunchroom just shrugged when I showed him what had happened....

Furiously, I was dabbing at my head, my neck—pulling off the peach bits....

On the playground, I kept patting at my hair, trying to hold it down, wanting school this day to be over....

And then:

"Hi!"

This was you, Kerry, on this day: Perfect blond curls bouncing all over your head. Bright blue eyes. Broad smile.

"Are you new to school?"

On this day I had fuzzy hair....

You didn't notice. You chattered away. Something had brought you across the playground, to stand before this new girl called Pat, and you were glowing....

"Those are cute shoes," you were saying, pointing to my new Capezio flats. "What color is that lipstick?" And "Did you like that English teacher?" And "When did you move to Northglenn?"

You had a million questions. A million more things to tell me.

So you weren't running from me, Kerry....

But you were saving me. And I watched you, talking to me and laughing matter-of-factly on that playground, and I could have knelt down on the ground and held you tight, and let the gratitude wash over me, even while I wanted not to need your human kindness.

At fourteen, I couldn't admit I needed it....

Thank you, Kerry Monroe.

This thing you did was a full thing. A God thing, maybe.

You never know what will happen when you walk into another person's life who has asked for or needs help. Maybe a God thing.

## CHAPTER 8

# BARNABAS AND YOU

◈

Here is the good news—the great news—of this book. Barnabas was used by God in extraordinary ways, and he *wasn't perfect*.

All of this talk about the Christlike attitudes of helping those who have failed or who are riding one of life's roller-coaster dips may come across as discouraging to ordinary Christians like you and me. It may sound like a proposal that we should become, that we should be, Jesus.

If that idea is now appearing like a billboard slogan in back of the words on this page, a clarification is in order. We don't have to be Jesus. We can settle for being a Barnabas. An actual, flawed, imperfect, limited human just like us.

In Galatians 2:13, after the triumph of the first missionary journey, Barnabas surprisingly caved in to peer pressure. He knew the truth of the gospel, that there was absolutely nothing—such as circumcision or even the Law of Moses—that could be added to simple faith in the Savior. And though he'd just traveled for months with Paul preaching the message of salvation by God's grace to Jews and Gentiles living in Asia Minor, the influence of

Barnabas's old Jewish friends still got to him. We can't be completely sure of what happened, but evidently Peter had shown up in Antioch, been drawn into the discussion led by a legalistic group on whether circumcision should be added as a requirement of faith, and he gave in. That probably was the final straw for Barnabas, who also gave in. We find out that Barnabas, as well as Peter, were still human. They continued to make mistakes after conversion.

Barnabas lived the kind of life that we can. He lived a life that was godly but real, with some foibles. That lifestyle is within our reach. It is doable.

Barnabas, then, is a biblical role model we can follow. He isn't so perfect that any of us can't imitate him. But a biblical question should haunt anyone who has read this far: Why, if Barnabas is such a model, are there so few people with his focus depicted in the New Testament? It's a fair question. And those who ask it should also ask a sibling query: When we get to the New Testament after the narratives of the Old, why do the number of bona fide superstars—Jesus, Paul—diminish and almost disappear? This is especially true after the book of Acts. After we read that far into the New Testament, there really is only Paul, who wrote more about the church and churches than about identifiable individuals.

All of the New Testament characters, like Barnabas, seem to fade out of the picture, back to the role of servant, helper, and…second placer. The New Testament reader might well wonder why. To be truthful, room is being made for only one person to take center stage. John said it well. "He must increase, but I must decrease." People like Barnabas don't claim center stage, and for good reason. Only one Person deserves that place.

## MAKING ROOM FOR JESUS

There is only one way to write about these truths. By telling stories. Stories of people who have lived as Barnabas lived. Making room for Jesus at the center stage of their lives by making room for others. "The King will reply, 'I tell you the truth, whatever you did for one of the least of these brothers of mine, you did for me.' " Who is "me" in this verse, or the "King"? It's Jesus. Who is "the least of these brothers of mine"? The unpopular, the uncared for, the unacknowledged, the unnoticed, the unimportant. Even today we consider these to be "the least"—the least favored, the least blessed, the least attractive, the least popular. It's not difficult to spot them.

In Philadelphia in the 1930s a young man grew up more under the guidance of his grandmother than his parents. His interests were typical of most young boys. But they didn't include church, until a man took an interest in him, a man whom the boy would in later years remember as a person who had oversized feet and a clumsiness about his ways. But the man believed in the boy. And every Sunday the boy would board a bus to go to the church where the man taught a boys' Sunday-school class. And the boy, drawn by the man's first kindnesses, began slowly to pay more and more attention to what was taught in class. He started studying the Bible sporadically and then more regularly. He grew up and attended seminary. Later he was asked to teach Bible at the seminary.

The little boy who became the seminary teacher is one of the most renowned leaders and Bible teachers in North America. Dr. Howard Hendricks is distinguished professor of Christian education and chairman of the Center for Christian Leadership at Dallas Theological Seminary. The pastors of many of this country's leading churches and the heads of major Christian organizations credit him as the significant model for their ministry skills and their motivation for a lifetime of service.

The church has benefited from these great teachers and pastors and leaders because of a clumsy Barnabas from Philadelphia with oversized feet.

Pastor and best-selling author Charles Swindoll, himself a student of Howard Hendricks, might have never made it in the ministry had there not been a Barnabas to encourage him in school. As a boy, he had a speech impediment. He was shy and struggled with speaking in public. Then he met a teacher who cared enough to not let him pass through that year without being given the chance to speak in class and move beyond the difficulty. Move beyond it he did.

One Barnabas who crossed my path probably doesn't remember the influence he had on me. It's been lasting. And I never worked for him or taught under him or served in an organization with him. That man is Ken Taylor, the founder and chairman of the board of Tyndale House Publishers.

In the Christian publishing business, Ken is known as the gravelly voiced older gentleman who travels to most national publishing conventions and there quietly encourages those who work for his company or for any Christian publishing company. He had a rocky start in the publishing business. He showed his thin *Living Letters* volume (his paraphrase of the New Testament) to as many as twenty publishers who turned him away. Although he was forced to publish it on his own, this paraphrase later joined its Old Testament counterpart and became *The Living Bible*, the most popular English paraphrase ever produced, and the foundation stone of Tyndale House Publishers. In the second half of the nineties, Tyndale published the apocalyptic Left Behind series of novels, the most widely read fiction ever to come out of a Christian publishing house.

So Ken Taylor has his accomplishments. But they did not affect me the way the man did.

In my first publishing job I ran into some difficulties that seemed insurmountable. With these troubles on my mind I attended a national book convention that first summer, unsure of whether I should continue in my editorial role or change companies or even quit the publishing business altogether.

The first morning of the convention, I took the elevator down to the floor with the hotel restaurant, which was already crowded with convention business. I looked over at the counter and saw a couple of empty stools. As I slid onto one of them I thought eating alone at a counter typified my life at that point.

As I waited for the cereal I had ordered, I looked around the restaurant and saw groups of fours and fives and sixes at their tables eagerly discussing marketing plans, the new relationships with a book distributor that had appeared almost overnight, and the speaker who would cap the convention in four days with his address.

Turning back toward my cornflakes that the waitress had just dropped off, I saw a gentleman peering at me from the front of the restaurant as if he had been looking for me. He made his way over and pulled himself onto the stool next to me, asking the waitress quietly for some toast and orange juice. After she left he turned to me, offered his hand, and stated his name so softly that I didn't catch it. But his manner was so sincere and gentle and godly that after a while I found myself talking with him about all sorts of things. I ultimately laid my problem before him using veiled names and asked him what I should do. His response was simple, with encouragement from the Bible for my situation and a concluding thought about how much the Lord loved me.

Our breakfast ended, he excused himself, and we parted company. Only later did I find out that the reason I could hardly hear him was because this was Ken Taylor, a man who had vocal cord trouble. I had eaten with one of the publishing giants, the paraphraser of *The Living Bible,* who never made any reference to his position or his place in our industry. I had prayed that morning. And God had sent Barnabas.

It happened again about ten years later. I was in an airport, waiting on a plane, when the thin, wispy-haired gentleman again came along and sat down beside me. This time I knew who he was. But he didn't want to talk about that. He was interested to hear about what I'd been doing, books I was excited about, and…if things were going well for me.

## OPPOSITE TO THE WORLD'S ATTITUDE

The Barnabas attitude doesn't get modeled for us every day. On the contrary. Its opposite is always in view.

Around the time I was writing this chapter, I boarded an airplane in Michigan to fly home. As I stood with my carry-on in the crowded Jetway leading to the plane's door, a few of us commented about the weather conditions. The storms had prevented some flights from keeping their schedules and had turned an air terminal on a Friday afternoon into a giant customer service center. Passengers hustled around, trading in tickets and finding seats on other airlines.

I asked a young lady standing behind me if she was going back home or just starting a trip. Striking in appearance in her tailored business suit, she spoke confidently. She told me that she went to school at a nearby college, a school I knew to have a Christian background.

"What are you majoring in?" I inquired.

"Political science and sociology," came the reply. By this time we had entered the plane through its forward door, made the corner into the first-class section, and I was dragging my black carry-on down the aisle trying to avoid the armrests that intermittently snagged my luggage straps.

"Sounds like the formula for a career in politics," I said, shoving the collapsible handle down into my bag. *Good,* I thought. *We need people like her representing Christ in the political arena.*

"I *love* Washington, D.C.," she said with enthusiasm, but also with an unmistakable seriousness. "I want to work there at some point. And I want to one day be the most powerful person there."

I almost fell over my suitcase.

I suppose we should expect to hear this line of thinking from our young people, our business community, and our leadership in a world where people seek guidance from presidents and senators instead of Jesus and his follower Barnabas. And yet there are those who bring the image of Barnabas, and the Spirit of Christ, alive every day. We can see them if we look.

On the same trip I talked with a woman who had never married but had three adopted children living with her. All three had mental difficulties and were passed over for adoption until she came along. I asked her why she did it. She knew they'd never have a chance to live in a real home unless she took them. She gave them the chance that others hadn't. Because she felt the Lord wanted her to. Barnabas lives.

I heard of another family who had two children affected by Down syndrome. These folks later became foster parents to two more similarly handicapped children. When someone told me about this couple, I wondered why they had taken on other challenging children. I'll never forget the answer. As their two children grew older and became more and more difficult to handle physically, the parents hired round-the-clock help to assist them in the lifting and carrying. As they settled into a manageable routine with their two children, the woman grew more and more convinced that other parents facing similar care challenges should be given the kind of aid that was so helpful to them. But this couple took that idea an extra step. Instead of just telling other families where to get that help, they decided to offer the help in an unusual way. The couple became foster parents to the handicapped children in two other families. They brought those children into their own home to live where the special care was already set up. The couple had a regular dorm with four special kids. Barnabas again.

Dr. Ben Carson, head of pediatric neurosurgery at Johns Hopkins University Hospital, performs operations on the brains of infants and children that enable these young people to grow up and live normal lives. He is an innovator, a worker of wonders, and a true hero. But you should hear him talk about one of his own heroes, a woman who sounds a lot like Barnabas. Norma Claypool is a single mother living in Baltimore. She has eight adopted children, all with severely deformed craniums that increase pressure on the brain with every day of growth. Dr. Carson plans to perform several surgeries on each child to reduce the deformities of their heads, surgeries without which they would die because of the ever-constricting bones in their heads. In between hospital visits, though, the children stay at their home—Norma's home—where she loves and hugs them as her own, children other people didn't want. What makes this Barnabas even more unusual is that Norma is blind.

It just takes one person acting in the role of a Barnabas to make *the* statement that someone hungers to hear. And when that person's head lifts up from their discouragement, any self-doubt about whether we have what it takes to be a Barnabas melts away.

By the way, did I mention job security in connection with the Barnabas Way? We'll always have a job. Someone's always in need of encouragement. And even better still, this enterprise doesn't require a large organization, or even a small one. All that any of us needs is a committee of one. And we can begin any day we want.

## CHAPTER 9

# A World Turned
# Upside Down

※

Certainly God does give us good things, what we call blessings. But not too many, and not always tangibly. "Our Father refreshes us on the journey with some pleasant inns, but will not encourage us to mistake them for home."

So then, how does this world, put together by God, work? What is God's way with us as far as blessings are concerned? Is he a rewarder? Is he arbitrary? Is he on our side? What should we expect from him? And he from us, in return?

## TIME TO ANTE UP

Every couple of weeks I get together with a friend who is one of my favorite conversationalists. Invariably our discussion gets around to how God acts in our lives. One week my friend believes God does it all— —and we are blessed, know it, and feel loved by God. Another week he will feel that God doesn't do much, and we make our own blessings through our God-given talents. Which is true? We can't have both. Or can we? Do we live in a world that is largely unblessed and hurting and in need of a touch of Christ—and that touch comes through us? Are we the blessing that God promises to others? And is it in blessing others that we receive our own blessing? Maybe we *can* have it both ways, but let's think about our own role first.

The motion picture *Glory*, set during the Civil War, follows the Union's all-black regiment, the 54th Massachusetts, into battle. The soldiers are commanded by a group of white officers, led by Captain Robert Gould Shaw, played by Matthew Broderick. One of the soldiers reporting to Shaw is Trip, played by Denzel Washington. The story centers on the training of the 54th, ultimately for an assault on Fort Wagner outside Charleston, a feat of bravery that the white Northern army didn't think a band of "coloreds" was up to. But the 54th was no contraband, disorganized, scavenging detachment of black soldiers. Their heroic, sacrificial assault on the South Carolina fort took the lives of two-thirds of the regiment in its courageous attack wave.

The day of the attack Shaw goes to Trip to ask him to carry the regimental flag, an honor Trip declines because he sees it as a sign that he's fighting for Shaw, for Northern whites, instead of for himself. This leads to a discussion about the war, its unfairness and Trip's belief that no one will win because they all will have to go back to their lives of poverty when the war ends. Sometimes we reach a similar conclusion when we look at the injustices in our world and the hurt some people go through and think ultimately that we don't really make a difference.

"I mean, what's the point," says Trip. "Ain't nobody goin' to win. It's just going to go on and on."

"It can't go on forever," replies Shaw.

"Yeah, but ain't nobody gonna win, sir," insists Trip.

"Somebody's gonna win," counters Shaw.

Trip still asks who's gonna win. He knows the white officers like Shaw will go back to the big houses they had before the war began. But men like Trip won't have anything to go back to. Shaw finally sees his point and wonders what they can do about this unfairness in life. Trip says everyone is guilty; they all have dirty hands. But it sure would be nice to get clean.

"How do we do that?" asks Shaw.

"We ante up and kick in, sir," says Trip.

The same is true today. It's time for us to ante up and kick in instead of just thinking that life is unfair and waiting, cap in hand, for God to send us the blessings that will solve our problems. Philip Yancey has talked about discovering the experience of spiritual blessing through living the Beatitudes. "We get abundant life by investing in others, standing for justice, ministering to the weak and needy, pursuing God, not self."

## THE UPSIDE-DOWN LIFE OF THE BLESSED

And so the way toward God is not found by calling down his blessings. The way toward God is toward...nonblessing. Toward those whose lives show little outward evidence of God's favor. Toward those who are hurting, broken, in need of a second chance. Toward those who have suffered violence or pain or who live in fear. Toward those who need relief, who need justice, who need a friend. By investing in these people, in God's name and power, we find that God goes with us. And so does his blessing.

We've hit the paradox again. Don't live for the blessing, waiting for it to arrive. But live for God, and for people in need, who are important to him—and God will be there in our lives, with his blessings. We don't ask for it, but then, like magic, it appears.

## THE PEOPLE GOD USES

There is no more surprising part of this paradoxical blessings experience than the unexpected array of people God uses.

I've mentioned my friend Mark, who has Huntington's Disease. The man is a walking laboratory in which God demonstrates his grace. Mark has a hard time not spilling his cup of coffee; he is sometimes hard to understand because of problems controlling the muscles with which he speaks; in our dates with him and his wife, we often allow extra time to get to a movie so a car can get picked up or an errand can be completed. But...I have never heard an unkind word out of Mark's mouth. About anyone. I have never heard him feel sorry for himself. When Mark and I go to a retreat or a movie, I think that I'm being something of a blessing to him, but Mark's life makes me want to be more like Jesus.

And Kim, Mark's wife, faces the uncertainties of the future

with their two children, Evan and Maddie. My wife and I thought we could offer her support and friendship. But what has resulted for us is a closeup view of a woman whose approach to life is a day-by-day reliance upon God, a demonstration of what waiting on God means for today and tomorrow but mostly for today, an example of what faith really means when lived out. And it has blessed us.

A friend of mine happens to be a literary agent as well as a lawyer. I sought for business purposes to establish good rapport with him, which isn't really difficult for all of us who know him. I guess this wasn't exactly being a blessing to him, but as our relationship developed, I got the chance to champion some of his authors and projects to our publishing house. He told me he appreciated the care I gave to those authors and their books.

One year my extended family faced court appearances because of a crime committed against us twenty years earlier. We were angry and frustrated over what would prove to be a useless prosecution, since the jury would ultimately reject the evidence as insufficient. I had to fly to another part of the country to attend the three-week trial.

At the midpoint of the trial, we knew we were losing. Added to that was the presence of reporters from tabloid news organizations who were broadcasting trial events, three writing teams devising proposals for book contracts, the producers of *Court TV,* and representatives from two major movie production firms. Our family wanted to protect our interests in the story that eventually would be told, knowing what can happen to plots and characters as screenwriters and directors put together a movie "based on a true story." We were feeling wronged by the court system and wronged by the media.

Then, out of nowhere, my friend showed up. He arrived with a knowledge of the judicial system that we didn't have. He suggested a type of registration that would protect our prior interests in the story, give us first claim to its commercial rights, and lay the groundwork for legal action we could pursue on the basis of privacy violations and libel. And he helped us and the other victim's family join our interests in a common legal agreement to prevent further exploitation by media and movie interests.

My friend gave my mother a great deal of comfort in providing legal recourse to what had been a feeding frenzy on the tragedies of my brother's and his friend's unsolved homicides. My friend did this for no fee. I had thought my work for his authors had been the blessing—but the blessing returned to me.

God can open the door for us into another person's life that is in need. We can then see how we can help. Some situations practically throw themselves at us. And they can come because of other members of our families. My kids have several friends who face troubling family problems, such as divorce. One day a group of kids was in our kitchen after school (we're one of the first homes on their route), and from my upstairs office I could clearly hear the second bag of chips and the second two-liter bottle of soda pop being opened. I went to my wife in another part of the house and suggested that we might begin charging admission at the front door.

"John," she said, "of the group of five who are here today,

three are in families where a divorce has occurred, one of which is still in process. You are the only man two of these kids will see today. Now, you can go in there and talk about them needing to purchase a ticket before entering our house, or you can go in there and be your usual, lovable, generous self and see if God might have a short appointment with a boy who'd like to talk to a man. About something other than the price of a bag of chips."

Two minutes later I was watching a computer skateboard program with the group and talking on the side with a guy about a go-ped. That night my son asked me why a certain couple got a divorce, since they're both Christians, and we ended up by talking about ways to encourage his friend.

Another kid from a single-parent home showed up at our house one night after dinner. He thought his parent would return in less than an hour, but he didn't feel comfortable staying in his house alone. The parent showed up three hours later. My younger son and our daughter emphasized again and again that he was welcome to stay longer at our house, even to stay the night. I had never seen such hospitality from those two, who told me later they wished their friend could have two parents so one could always be at home.

## IT ISN'T AS WE THINK

I cited Albert Einstein at the beginning of this book. The universe in which he lived—in which we live—isn't operating as we think it should, according to science and physics as we understand them. Einstein postulated the existence of *antigravity* to explain some of the irregularities, but scientists weren't listening. According to scientists, the universe, after its "Big Bang" beginning, should be slowing down in its rush away from the bang's center as it spreads out over time. But because of data from space telescopes like Hubble, we find out the exact opposite is happening. The universe is speeding up in its journey to wider and wider reaches of space, almost as if something is pushing it. Einstein was right. Things are not as we think they should be.

As Christians in the tradition of Barnabas and Jesus, we do the opposite of what the world thinks is right. Instead of seeking to work with the strong, the independent, and the powerful, we work with those in need, those who don't stand out, and those who want a friend. But a turnaround may await us in heaven:

It is a serious thing to live in a society of possible gods and goddesses, to remember that the dullest and most uninteresting person you can talk to may one day be a creature which, if you saw it now, you would be strongly tempted to worship, or else a horror and a corruption such as you now meet, if at all, only in a nightmare. All day long we are, in some degree, helping each other to one or the other of these destinations. It is in the light of these overwhelming possibilities, it is with the awe and the circumspection proper to them, that we should conduct all our dealings with one another, all friendships, all loves, all play, all politics. There are no *ordinary* people. You have never talked to a mere mortal. Nations, cultures, arts, civi-

lizations—these are mortal, and their life is to ours as the
life of a gnat. But it is immortals whom we joke with,
work with, marry, snub, and exploit—immortal horrors
or everlasting splendours. (Emphasis added.)

We may not always have the perspective that each person we
meet is being fitted for immortality in one fashion or another.
But here are a few other perspective questions. When we believe
in someone who has failed, who is the person who really starts to
succeed? When we give a chance to a person who needs a second
one, who starts to get lucky? When we help the hurting, who else
begins to heal? When we take on a "loser," who wins? Ours is a
business that may promise little or no return at first, but it is followed by the best return long-term, for us *and* for those we find
and who find us. "There is a promise in the future of health and
peace—but not now. To people who are trapped in pain, in broken homes, in economic chaos, in hatred and fear, in violence—
to these Jesus offers a promise of a time, far longer and more
substantial than this time on earth, of health and wholeness and
pleasure and peace. A time of reward."

The Barnabas Way leads us to the best job in the world; it is
when we feel most alive. C. S. Lewis believed that becoming a little
Christ and being presented by Christ to the Father is the only thing
we were made for. I have a similar feeling about the Barnabas Way.
When it's all said and done, the times that mean the most—that
we feel we are doing the thing we were made for—are going to be
the times we've reached out to those God wants us to help.

## A SOLUTION FOR EVERYTHING?

By now it is clear that I didn't choose to write a book only about a New Testament character named Barnabas. This is a book about people helping other people. About Christians helping others whether they are Christians or Hindus or those of the Islamic faith or those with no faith whatsoever.

A few weeks before I finished writing this book, three commercial jetliners were hijacked and flown into the World Trade Center towers and the Pentagon by radical extremists. We live in a new world since that day. We fly on planes and glance around the cabin to see if anyone looks as though they will get up from their seat and rush the cockpit. We go to the subway or get on a bus, and we dread more than anticipate the trip. We look at the food in our stores and the letters in our mailbox and wonder if they've been tampered with. We are even afraid of the air we breathe, wondering what toxin or poison can be disguised by its invisibility.

We have become less trusting of those who walk among us. And that distrust leads to a hesitancy about humanity that makes us not want to step forward toward people as we should. What can be said to quell the hate that began this downward spiral?

Maybe nothing can be said. But maybe something can be *done*. I don't know any global answers for terrorism, hate, and a radical commitment to eradicating those who believe differently—the supreme commitment to intolerance. I don't know how nations and peoples can coexist with others as the hysterical crowds whip up "death to" chants and mobs rule the emotions of people.

But I do know one thing we can all do. And that's to do the things Barnabas would do, one act of kindness at a time, for people who need a second chance, a new beginning, some hope. Ephesians 2:10 says we are God's greatest work—our lives, our marriages, our families, our vocations, our discipleship. It is these he has given us, put us into, and caused us to be a part of to show off the good works that lead people to him.

## The Glory of Being Second

Words about second placers, and their role as those Barnabas takes on, are somewhat misleading. Because *second placers* is a label that applies to more than them. It applies to you and me. We're all second placers.

How do I know? Growing up, in my schoolwork, in the sports I played, I can't ever remember a time when someone else (or many someone elses) didn't stand in line in front of me. I ran my first 10K last year, an event in Boulder, Colorado. I just dug out the computer printout for the race, the one personalized with my stats. Out of 41,117 finishers (it's the country's fifth largest road race), and out of 19,218 male finishers, I came in 7,020th. In my age group—forty-nine—I finished 384th. Observation: I notice no number ones in any of those statistics.

But the thing I can come in first place at doing, and the thing all of us can come in first place doing, is reaching out to the non-blessed, those who maybe need a break or a friend, or both. He or she represents a potential win. And their win is ours.

## AN IMPOSSIBLE MESSAGE

I know this book in many ways proclaims an impossible message. There isn't anyone who can be Barnabas to every person he or she meets. I don't think God intended that. The inclusion of John Mark and Paul in the biblical record instead of an additional fifteen more like them says something about the room one can make in one's life for helping others.

But Barnabas is a worthy model for all of us. Blessings will be ours as we serve others. And we'd be hard pressed to find a better way to spend our time. We are princesses kissing frogs so that others may see they've never been frogs at all. We do that which will last forever in adding to God's kingdom. And we say along with Jewel, the talking unicorn in C. S. Lewis's *The Last Battle*, in response to the wish that Narnia could last forever, "Nay, sister, all worlds draw to an end, except Aslan's own country." It is Aslan's country we are headed for, and the happy ending each of us has dreamed of. For happy endings are hoped for the world over.

Barnabas showed us how to come alongside those who are hurting or in need and start walking with them toward a happier ending. One day, along with those we've encouraged and those who've encouraged us, we will at last begin to live in that place where all tears will be wiped away and where there will be no more death or mourning or crying or pain. And we will live forever that ending we have all been looking for.

# Notes

## Introduction

*page*

1    *1975 movie: The Man Who Would Be King*, directed by
John Huston, screenplay by John Huston and Gladys Hill,
Allied Artists/Columbia Pictures Corporation, Hollywood,
1975.

2    *Lewis:* C. S. Lewis, *The Problem of Pain* (San Francisco: Harper-
SanFrancisco, 2001), 40.

3    *Remain true to the Lord:* See Acts 11:23.

4    *"A good man":* Acts 11:24.

4    *Pure in heart:* "Blessed are the pure in heart, for they will see
God" (Matthew 5:8). "Blessed are the merciful, for they will be
shown mercy" (Matthew 5:7).

4    *This person is blessed:* From the *NIV Bible Commentary*, electronic
version, Kenneth Barker and John Kohlenberger III, consulting
editors. Entry 149 of 204 on the word "blessed." A part of
*Zondervan Reference Software* (22-bit edition), Version 26
(Grand Rapids: Zondervan, 1994).

# CHAPTER 1

*page*

5   *Yancey:* Philip Yancey, *The Jesus I Never Knew* (Grand Rapids: Zondervan, 1995), 76-7.

5   *"We want, in fact":* C. S. Lewis, *The Problem of Pain* (San Francisco: HarperSanFrancisco, 2001), 31.

10   *Lewis:* C. S. Lewis, *Mere Christianity* (New York: HarperCollins, 1980), 42.

11   Hoosiers: *Hoosiers,* directed by David Anspaugh, screenplay by Angelo Pizzo. Hemdale Film Corporation; Orion Pictures, Hollywood, 1987.

13   *Yancey:* Yancey, *The Jesus I Never Knew,* 113.

# CHAPTER 2

*page*

15   *"Men are mirrors":* C. S. Lewis, *Mere Christianity* (New York: HarperCollins, 1980), 190.

16   *"Altogether upside down":* Russell Sparks, editor, *Prophet of Orthodoxy: The Wisdom of G. K. Chesterton* (London: HarperCollins/ Fount, 1993), 188.

16   *"Are more satisfying":* Cited by Sparks, *Prophet of Orthodoxy,* 190.

16   *Lewis:* C. S. Lewis, *The Problem of Pain* (San Francisco: Harper-SanFrancisco, 2001), 28.

16 *God's paradoxical conclusions:* Robert Farrar Capon, *The Parables of the Kingdom* (Grand Rapids: Eerdmans, 1985), 63.

16 *Long, slow curve:* Capon, *The Parables of the Kingdom,* 20.

22 *How to deal with all of them:* J. Madeleine Nash, "Einstein's Unfinished Symphony," *Time* (New York: Time, Inc., 11 December 1999), 83-7.

23 *Buford:* Bob Buford, *Halftime* (Grand Rapids: Zondervan, 1994).

23 *Muzikowski:* Bob Muzikowski, *Safe at Home* (Grand Rapids: Zondervan, 2001).

24 *"The Beatitudes reveal":* Philip Yancey, *The Jesus I Never Knew* (Grand Rapids: Zondervan, 1995), 117.

## CHAPTER 3

*page*

29 *Halberstam:* David Halberstam, *The Best and the Brightest* (New York: Random House, 1972).

31 *"Such awful people":* C. S. Lewis, *Mere Christianity* (New York: HarperCollins, 1980), 213.

32 Shrek: *Shrek,* directed by Andrew Adamson and Vicky Jenson, DreamWorks SKG, Universal City, Calif., 2001. Based on a book by Ted Elliot and Terry Rossio; screenplay by Joe Stillman and Roger S. H. Schulman.

33 *Campbell:* Will Campbell, *Brother to a Dragonfly* (New York: Continuum, 2000), 217-22.

35 *As Shakespeare wrote:* "The fault, dear Brutus, is not in our stars, But in ourselves, that we are underlings" (*Julius Caesar,* I, ii, 140-1).

## CHAPTER 4

*page*

39 *Later the church named Barnabas:* See Acts 13:1; 14:14.

40 *"[He] sold a field":* Acts 4:37.

40 *Inherited property:* Richard N. Longenecker, *The Expositor's Bible Commentary,* vol. 9, Frank E. Gaebelein, editor (Grand Rapids: Zondervan, 1981), 312.

40 *Believers in Jerusalem:* See Acts 4:32-33.

41 *Barnabas defended this man:* See Acts 9:27.

42 *The letters would have enabled:* See Acts 9:1-2.

42 *It was a meeting that changed:* See Acts 9:3-22.

42 *Stand in the gap:* See Acts 9:26-28.

42 *Barnabas again came forward:* See Acts 11:25-26.

45 *The third and largest section:* See Acts 11:25-30; 12:25; 13:1-52; 14:1-28; 15:1-41.

45 *First missionary journey:* See Acts 13–14.

47 *Barnabas wanted to keep John Mark:* See Acts 13:13; 15:36-41.

47 *His arm around a failure:* See Acts 15:39.

49 *Their work in Jerusalem together:* See 1 Corinthians 9:6; Galatians 2:1,9.

49 *A fellow worker:* See Colossians 4:10; 2 Timothy 4:11; Philemon 24.

# CHAPTER 5

*page*

52  *Sermon on the Mount:* See Matthew 5–7.

53  *Beatitudes:* See Matthew 5:3-12.

57  *Barnabas actually began:* See Acts 13:1-3.

57  *Barnabas and Paul served equally:* See Acts 13–14.

57  *"He must become greater":* John 3:30.

58  *"Give preference to one another":* Romans 12:10, NASB.

58  *"Honor one another":* Romans 12:10.

59  *Lystra:* See Acts 14:8-18.

61  *"Comforts us in all our troubles":* 2 Corinthians 1:4.

61  *Yancey:* Philip Yancey, *The Jesus I Never Knew* (Grand Rapids: Zondervan, 1995), 22, 147-9.

# CHAPTER 6

*page*

65-7  *Rudy Ruettiger:* Adapted from the film *Rudy,* directed by David Anspaugh, screenplay by Angelo Pizzo, Columbia TriStar, Culver City, Calif., 1993; as well as Rudy Ruettiger, Cheryl Ruettiger, and Rebecca Atkinson, *Rudy's Lessons for Young Champions* (Henderson, Nev.: Rudy International, 1997). See also Rudy Ruettiger and Mike Celizic, *Rudy's Rules* (Waco, Tex.: WRS Publishing, 1995).

68  *Those who study human behavior:* Two men often cited for their work related to understanding human motivation are Abraham Maslow and Clayton P. Alderfer. These books are considered their

most important works: Maslow, *Motivation and Personality* (New York: Harper & Row, 1954); Maslow, *The Farther Reaches of Human Nature* (New York: Penguin, 1971); Alderfer, *Existence, Relatedness, and Growth* (New York: Free Press, 1972).

69 *What makes us ultimately:* Educational Psychology Interactive: Maslow's hierarchy of needs, found at http://chiron.valdosta.edu/whuitt/col/regsys/maslow.html.

70 *There is a diagram:* Bill Bright, "Have You Heard of the Four Spiritual Laws?" (Orlando: Campus Crusade for Christ, 1965).

71 *Yet seventeen million adult Americans:* National Institute of Mental Health, cited in APA Online (American Psychological Association), found at http://www.apa.org.

72 *Recommended suggestions:* Depression Info Center, Continuing Medical Education Association, © 1995–2001 CME, Inc., found at http://www.mhsource.com/depression.

## CHAPTER 7

*page*

77-8 *Strep to salmonella:* Andrea Dorfman, "Potions from Poisons," *Time* (New York: Time, Inc., 15 January 2001), 96-9.

81 *Modern authors portray Jesus:* Philip Yancey, *The Jesus I Never Knew* (Grand Rapids: Zondervan, 1995), 19.

81 *Some professional athletes see Jesus:* Yancey, *The Jesus I Never Knew,* 19.

82 *Nouwen:* Author and priest Henri Nouwen taught at the University of Notre Dame, the Catholic Theological Institute in Utrecht, Yale Divinity School, and Harvard Divinity School.

82  *Adam:* Henri Nouwen, *Adam: God's Beloved* (Maryknoll, N.Y.: Orbis, 1997).

84-6  *Raybon:* Patricia Raybon, *My First White Friend* (New York: Penguin, 1996), 85-96.

## CHAPTER 8

*page*

89  *"He must increase":* John 3:30, NASB.

89  *"The King will reply":* Matthew 25:40.

95  *Norma Claypool:* Adapted from *Gifted Hands: The Ben Carson Story* on video. Produced by Cal Covert, Jan van den Bosch. © 1992 Zondervan, Ben Carson.

## CHAPTER 9

*page*

97  *"Our Father refreshes":* C. S. Lewis, *The Problem of Pain* (San Francisco: HarperSanFrancisco, 2001), 116.

98-9  Glory: *Glory,* directed by Edward Zwick, screen-play by Kevin Jarre, Columbia Tri-Star, Culver City, Calif., 1989.

99  *"We get abundant life":* Philip Yancey, *The Jesus I Never Knew* (Grand Rapids: Zondervan, 1995), 125.

104  *As if something is pushing it:* Michael D. Lemonick, "Einstein's Repulsive Idea," *Time* (New York: Time, Inc., 16 April 2001), 58-9.

104-5   *"It is a serious thing"*: C. S. Lewis, *The Weight of Glory and Other Addresses* (San Francisco: HarperSanFrancisco, 1949, 1976, 1980), 45-6.

105   *"There is a promise"*: Yancey, *The Jesus I Never Knew,* 113.

105   *Lewis:* C. S. Lewis, *Mere Christianity* (New York: HarperCollins, 1980), 200.

108   *"Nay, sister"*: C. S. Lewis, *The Last Battle,* bk. 7, *The Chronicles of Narnia* (New York: HarperCollins, 1956), 101.

108   *No more death:* Revelation 21:4.

# ACKNOWLEDGMENTS

I want to mention a few people by name who, since my days in graduate school, have inspired the central idea of this book, even though none of them have been aware of this. I didn't know a book on the subject would ever result. But now that it has, I want to write a note about their influence.

Dr. Howard Hendricks was the first person who taught me that there was someone other than Paul in Acts 9–15. He also taught that truth has to be lived to be truth, not just examined or studied or preached. Prof's stories about people like the Sunday-school teacher with big feet kept seminary classes from being sterile laboratories and always put a lump in my throat. Being on the open road the way Barnabas was, I wonder if Barnabas could have hung in there with as many guys needing a second chance as are found on a seminary campus. Seminary is the hothouse where the Encourager named Prof. Hendricks has chosen to live to help us second chancers thrive.

In 1979 Chuck Swindoll didn't know that I took my first publishing house job so I could edit him. We've known each other for over twenty years, and even though I've heard many messages in which he's encouraged his wide audience, he's always been available to encourage on the personal side. Always. Chuck, Son of Encouragement.

Philip Yancey writes books that probe the mind and take on the tough questions no Christian wants to have to answer. Struggling with those questions instead of acting as if they don't exist, Philip encourages the skeptic in many of us that God has answers—or something better than answers—for life's toughest dilemmas and darkest mysteries. Philip's wife, Janet, works in all kinds of situations that most of us would not choose, from the inner city to hospice care facilities. With their background and insight, Philip and Janet have a unique perspective on the subject of encouragement.

While I was putting together the final chapters of this book, I informed the Yanceys that my wife and I were trying to help a family whose domestic situation had actually become life threatening for some members. Philip and Janet encouraged us and commended us, then Philip did something I wasn't expecting. He offered monetary resources to help if it was appropriate. The only string attached was that we would just say yes. Some people talk about helping and encouraging. Some write about it. The Yanceys live it.

My friends Dan Rich and Ron Lee believed in this book when it was an idea. They have lived that belief in front of others, affirming that "encouragement" is a response we can give at any time in any situation. It's often more important than the blessings we hope for. Ron's and Dan's insights and help have made this a better book.

Living the truth, being willing to be personally involved, struggling with some of life's toughest dilemmas—those traits of character that you see in the examples above are a wonderful demonstration of the way of Barnabas. And they are wonderfully brought to life by another person I want to acknowledge: my wife. Laren said when I first mentioned the concept of this book, "John, *you* do that." I do it some. But Laren has done it ever since I've known her. She has lived it before me. Without her, I would have never found the Barnabas Way.

# ABOUT THE AUTHOR

John Sloan is an editor with Zondervan Publishing House, a subsidiary of HarperCollins Publishers. He has worked in the publishing business for more than twenty years with numerous authors and writers. He currently lives in Colorado with his wife and their three children.